NEEDLEPOINT MINIATURES

SUSAN HIGGINSON

Alphabooks

First published in 1987 by Alphabooks Ltd.,
Sherborne, Dorset, England

ISBN 0 906670 47 0 (hardback)
    0 906670 45 4 (paperback)

British Library Cataloguing in Publication Data

Higginson, Susan
    Needlepoint miniatures.
    1. Canvas embroidery—Patterns
    I. Title
    746.44'2041   TT.778.C3

    ISBN 0-906670-47-0
    ISBN 0-906670-45-4 Pbk

Printed by Gildenprint Ltd, Bristol
Bound by Hunter and Foulis, Edinburgh
Typeset by Margaret Spooner Typesetting, London SE15

Acknowledgements

I should like to thank my family for their help
and encouragement during the writing of this
book, also Lawrie Hopkins for his efficient and
friendly framing service and my students for
their enthusiastic interest. Colour photography
of all the original designs was undertaken by
Edward Piper. The pictures on pages 6, 7 and
8 are by courtesy of the Victoria & Albert
Museum, London. The lower picture on page
12 is of work by Heather Prescott. The design
for 'Lake scene' on page 26 is from a range of
cards designed by Trudi Finch.

CONTENTS

INTRODUCTION

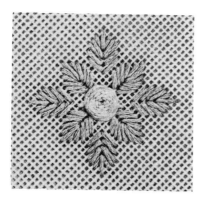

Small things have a fascination all their own, and miniatures in needlepoint are no exception. Of all the pieces of work on show in my needlepoint studio, new students invariably gravitate to the corner where the miniatures hang and say, longingly, 'How long will it be before I can do one of those? That is what I would really like to make.'

In essence, of course, it is no more difficult to design a tiny needlepoint picture and work it in silks than it is to make a large cushion in wools; but because the miniatures must be worked on a small-mesh canvas to be at all effective, they are not ideal subjects for beginners just learning the stitches for the first time.

The range of stitches used in landscape miniatures is not as great as that used in more general work, as many of the square stitches are not suitable for such projects, but the full range comes into play in the other types of miniatures featured in this book. Much of the fun in needlepoint comes from the enormous variety of stitches which can be used, and as the stitch directory at the end of the book shows, most of the common, and many of the uncommon, stitches have been incorporated into the designs. Also included are general chapters on sources of inspiration, design and materials necessary, as well as a chapter which shows different ways of depicting common features such as trees, brick and stonework, skies and fields, some of which may not have appeared in the worked examples.

In this book I want to share with you the results of many hours of trial and much error, and I feel that the best way of doing this is through a series of examples which are described in great detail, with all the possible pitfalls clearly signposted, so that when you come to design your own projects you will know how to go about it. Once you have worked one or two of the examples, I expect you will not be able to open a magazine or look at a landscape without seeing endless ideas for future projects. Translating your ideas into reality will give you a great deal of pleasure, and your family and friends will treasure the finished products — if you can bear to part with them.

Not one but two 'frogges', above, and, right, an
elephant embroidered in silk by Mary Queen of
Scots and Bess of Hardwicke, *c.* 1570, in cross stitch.
Part of the Oxburgh Hangings.

1
NEEDLEPOINT
IN HISTORY

Needlepoint, which can also be referred to as canvas work, is a very old craft, with some examples dating back to the thirteenth and fourteenth centuries. It is a type of stitchery on an openweave ground which developed from and alongside the more free-flowing embroidery practised on closely woven fabrics. Unlike other forms of needlework, needlepoint usually completely covers the background material with either a single stitch or a variety of different stitches. It thus forms a very strong and textured fabric which can be put to many and varied uses.

Needlepoint had its original burst of popularity in the first Elizabethan age, when both amateur and professional needlewomen produced a vast number of intricately worked designs, such as the Bradford Table Carpet (detail on page 8) and the Oxburgh Hangings (as shown here, and in the adapted elephant design on page 62). In an age when decorative possibilities were limited, needlepoint cushions, book covers and hangings were considered essential in every

well-to-do household. Despite the fact that many of these items were enormous, the range of stitches was very limited, and the favourite stitch was the smallest one of all, tent stitch.

During the centuries that followed, fashions changed, and gradually, as new furnishing materials were introduced and became generally available, the popularity of needlepoint as a furnishing medium declined and standards became very low. During Victorian times there was, however, a revival of interest in canvas work with the introduction of Berlin Wool Work. In this type of needlepoint, designs were copied from squared sheets and worked in the newly available aniline dyed wools, the colours of which were harsh and crude. The Victorian ladies had much leisure for their craft, but the designs they followed were often tasteless and uninteresting.

After the Second World War new approaches were made to needlepoint as to many other crafts. The constraints of the past were thrown off and much experimentation is

7

now taking place. There is much more use of abstract designs and many pieces of work, as is the case with the pictures in this book, are made for purely decorative purposes. The greatest advance in this new Elizabethan age of needlepoint has been in the realm of the stitches used. The sixteenth-century needlewoman would be amazed, and probably horrified, by some of the stitches used in the designs which follow. Obviously they would have been unsuited to her purposes, as they are often three-dimensional and would be quite out of place on a chair seat or table carpet. They do, however, make the craft of needlepoint very much more interesting, and with so many beautiful stitches at one's fingertips the designing of projects such as the miniatures featured in this book becomes a pleasure not to be missed. The designs in this book were made to hang on the wall, framed, like paintings or photographs, but there are many other ways both practical and decorative in which they could be used.

A detail from the Bradford Table Carpet in the Victoria & Albert Museum, London, embroidered in tent stitch in the sixteenth century.

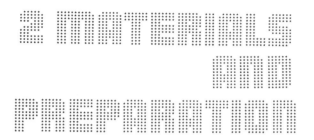

2 MATERIALS AND PREPARATION

One of the advantages of working miniatures is that material costs are kept to a minimum — a metre of canvas goes a long way when you are only using pieces less than six inches square for each project.

The following guide lines will help you to choose your materials and make the necessary preparation for working.

Canvas

The basic material on which these miniatures are worked is canvas, familiar to all needlepoint workers. To achieve any degree of detail in the limited compass of these tiny projects, a small-mesh single (mono) canvas must be used. The worked examples are all stitched on 18s (18 thread-to-the-inch), but a smaller mesh could be used if you find it comfortable to work with. You do have to have very good eyesight to work with anything smaller than 18s, unless you use a magnifying lens.

White canvas is more suitable for this work than brown, in that if it is placed over a design the lines of the design will show through clearly and can be marked straight on to the canvas. This cannot be so easily done with the brown canvas. This apart, white canvas should be used if your project needs mainly pale-coloured threads, and brown or ecru if darker threads are being used; any canvas showing through the design is thus less obvious.

The finished product will not receive a great deal of wear and a lightweight interlock canvas is quite adequate. This type of canvas, where the vertical thread divides round each horizontal thread and locks it firmly into place, is useful in that the edges do not fray and the mesh stays in place as you work — important when the stitches are so small. Its

Packets of Madeira threads.

disadvantage is that sometimes the cheaper canvases are not of very high quality. Make sure that the threads are smooth and the whole is free from knots.

If you want to try one of the designs in the book on a larger scale, this is perfectly easy. The outline drawings can be enlarged on a photocopier, or the simpler ones copied by eye straight on to a larger-mesh canvas, 13s or 14s perhaps. You would then use crewel wool or Persian yarn and a size 20 tapestry needle.

Working threads

The Madeira brand of six-stranded mercerised cotton is eminently suitable; the convenient sealed packs prevent the strands from getting knotted up as they are pulled out, and the cover keeps the cotton clean. There are ten metres (33 ft) of thread in a pack. However, similar materials are made by a number of companies, and can be substituted if Madeira is not available. The whole six strands of the complete thread are normally used; occasionally fewer strands are needed, perhaps for French knot flowers or shading on top of another colour. Sometimes two shades are mixed in the needle (in any number of strands not exceeding six) to achieve special effects. Metallic threads can be used for highlights, but sparingly.

What to do if the canvas shows through the stitching Sometimes, with long straight stitches, the thread may not cover the canvas very well. Unless this is so marked that you need to insert more strands, the remedy is to untwist the cotton thread as you work. This will make the thread lie over a wider area and will increase its lustrous effect. Another remedy, if the canvas is going to show behind the threads, is to colour the canvas before stitching with a matching colour. This should be done with either dryish acrylic paints or a *waterproof* fibre-tipped pen. If you colour too much canvas the whiteness may be restored by judicious use of typewriter correcting fluid.

Needles

Tapestry needles size 22 are the best for this work if it is done on 18s canvas. To test whether your needle is the correct size for the canvas you are using, drop the needle into one of the holes, with the eye diagonally across the hole; if it falls straight through it is too small, if it distorts the shape of the hole greatly on being pulled through, it is too large. The correct size needle can be pulled gently through with hardly any distortion of the canvas hole.

Preparing the canvas for use

Cut a piece of canvas the size of the finished article plus about one inch (2.5 cm) all round. This should then be bound with a well-sticking masking tape to prevent your threads catching on the edges as you sew. An example is shown on page 41.

Using a frame

As the pieces of canvas are so small it is quite easy to hold them in the hand for working. If, however, you like using a frame you will probably have to adapt one of the round embroidery frames for your use, as there are few needlepoint frames on the market small enough for miniatures. It would distort the canvas to hold it between the rings of a round frame, so stretch either a piece of fine canvas or a piece of firmly woven fabric over the frame, and then cut a hole in the middle of

this fabric of such a size that you are able to sew your canvas to this fabric (with back stitch), while also being able to get at the back of your design to work it.

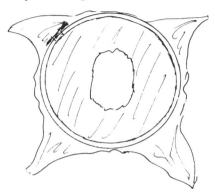

When adapting a round embroidery frame, first cut a hole in the fabric, slightly larger than the area to be embroidered (as above), and then sew your canvas over the hole (as below).

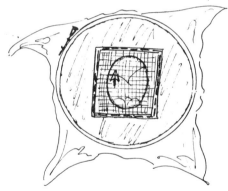

If you do not use a frame, try nevertheless to keep the canvas flat, and do not handle the worked area unduly as this can spoil the lustre of the threads.

Other materials which should be available

scissors a large pair for cutting the canvas, a small pair with sharp blades and points for the threads

pencils, rubbers, fibre-tipped pens for designing and drawing on the canvas

magnifying glass if you have tired eyes

masking tape one with good sticking qualities, from a DIY or hardware store

If you are designing a landscape miniature of your own, either out of your imagination or using something like a watercolour painting as the basis, there are two main things to remember. Firstly, no more detail must be put in than can satisfactorily be shown in stitches at this scale, and secondly, although some small details can be worked and do look very effective, there must be large enough areas of the majority of the stitches to show them off to advantage. You are, after all, designing a *needlepoint* picture, and as the range of stitches is so vast it would be a pity to make your design so complex that you were forced to use tent stitch for most of the work. Avoid, therefore, things such as wrought iron gates with lots of scrollwork, trees with tendril-like branches, ships with complicated rigging, and so on. If your design absolutely requires something of this nature, it is better to work a background of stitches and then embroider your narrow lines on top, as, for example, the smoke in 'Thatched cottage' (see page 32).

The tendency is always to feel that a very simple picture will be uninteresting, and if it were to be coloured in flat poster colours then perhaps it would be; but the interest is in the stitch patterns and the play of light on the silks just as much as in the subject matter, so to begin with, the simpler the better.

Stylizing

Needlepoint pictures of this kind are by their nature very stylized, and little attempt is made to achieve an entirely naturalistic result. Various features, such as houses and animals, are often made very much out of proportion with their background, especially if they are the main subjects. Nevertheless, it is a good idea to make a distinction in the size of the stitches chosen for foreground and background areas, using the larger ones in the front of the picture; also, paler colours should be used for hills or other features which form the further points of the scene.

Drawing the design and transferring it to the canvas

Draw your simple design on plain paper and go over it with a dark fibre-tipped pen. Place the prepared piece of canvas over the drawing and with a sharp HB pencil or pale-coloured waterproof marker, trace the design on to the canvas. If using pencil do not make your lines too dark, or the lead may come off on the threads. Waterproof markers are preferable but care must be taken to make only light lines, as otherwise they may show through between straight stitches.

Points to note If your design includes features such as houses with windows, you will have to take into account the fact that the mesh of the canvas may prevent your putting the lines exactly where you want them. For example, if you are working a house with regularly placed

11

four-pane windows, you will have to decide on the number of threads to allow for the windows, the window frames and the spaces in between the windows. It is unlikely you will be able to match the needlepoint picture exactly with the original idea, so a little juggling has to take place to get an effect which is a close match. Hints on how to deal with this sort of problem are given in the chapter on Special Effects, on page 16.

You must also leave yourself some leeway for altering the design as you sew, since the picture, as it grows on the canvas, often looks rather different from how you envisaged it originally. For instance, depending on what stitch you choose, the shape of a tree or group of trees will probably not fit exactly inside the shape you have drawn for it, so the design should be such that this will not matter.

Certain stitches suit certain subjects. Diagonal stitches are good for the sky, as in the seascape below, while a variety of different stitches is used in the house design to indicate masonry, brickwork, slate and wood.

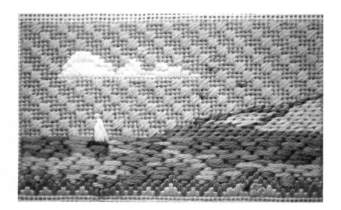

Choosing the stitches

There are, including variations, hundreds of different needlepoint stitches, so choosing just six or eight for a small picture might seem a rather daunting prospect. However, as you become familiar with the more commonly used stitches, you will find that you have your favourites, and you will certainly feel that some stitches are much more suitable for certain subjects than others. For instance, diagonal stitches seem appropriate for the sky of any picture — thinking of rays of light or rain falling on the earth. For sloping hillsides, again a diagonal stitch often seems right, matching the angle of the hillside as nearly as possible. If a pattern of fields is being built up, then a good variety of different textures is called for. The stitches most suitable for buildings depend entirely on what the building is made of — patterns of bricks and stone, whitewashed walls or wood all require different treatment. Similarly slate, tile and thatched roofs can all be suggested by stitchery.

Detailed descriptions of stitches for all sorts of different situations are given in the chapter on Special Effects, on page 16.

Choosing the colours

However well you have designed your picture and however skilfully you have worked your stitches, if you have chosen colours which do not suit your subject the final effect will be disappointing. The golden rule is that you should not use too many colours in one miniature, probably five main colours is about right, and these should blend together pleasingly. It is best to choose several from the same colour group on the shade card so that they tone well together. In a real landscape there are very few bright colours, so the reds and bright pinks are best kept to the occasional small highlight. Always have one or two fairly neutral colours in a picture, so that the whole is not too 'busy' with nowhere for the eye to rest.

Working with stranded cottons

All the stranded cottons are slightly twisted when you buy them, but their lustre shows to better effect if the threads lie parallel in the worked stitches. Some needleworkers recommend dividing the working threads into the six separate strands, laying them parallel, then threading them together into the needle. Certainly try this way and see if it works well for you, but it is very difficult to get the strands together again evenly, and the stitches then look worse instead of better!

The method used here is as follows: when starting a new length of thread, run your fingers sharply down it several times to flatten it out, and then unravel it slightly before threading the needle. As the stitching progresses, constantly untwist the thread which tends to twist up as it moves backwards and forwards through the canvas.

Use lengths of thread not longer than 14 inches (40 cms) and only push about 2 inches (5 cms) through the eye. Do not thereafter move the cotton in the eye, and when you have worked as far as you can with this length, finish off the thread. If you try to use the thread in your picture which has been in the eye of the needle, you will find that it is slightly frayed and has lost most of its lustre.

Helpful hints

1 Always use 'stab' stitch when working needlepoint, i.e. push the needle vertically through the canvas to the back, and pull all the thread through before putting the needle in again to come out to the front of the work. This might sometimes seem a slow method, but it keeps the canvas stiff and in good shape and means that the resulting stitches are very even.

2 When starting a new thread, never make a knot. Hold about ½ inch (1.2 cms) of thread along the back of the work and sew over it. When there is a surface of cotton on the back near where you are working, run the new thread through this for about ½ inch (1.2 cm). Similarly, finish off a thread by running about ½ inch (1.2 cms) through stitches on the back of the work, then cut off the thread flush. Do not leave loose ends.

3 If possible, always work *up* through an empty hole and *down* into one already used. This prevents frayed ends coming through from the back. Of course, this is not possible when you have to go into one hole many times.

4 The selvedge of canvas, as with other materials, is designed to be placed at the *side* of the work, but with interlock canvas, especially in such tiny pieces, this is not relevant. For the miniatures in this book it has been found most satisfactory to use the canvas with the selvedge at the *top*, as the mesh is very slightly narrower this way and the threads cover better.

5 It might be helpful to make your own shade card for each project. On a small piece of card write the Madeira shade number, or other identifying reference, and alongside each number stick a short length of the colour being used.

Working the picture

It is not always easy, when beginning to work on these tiny landscapes, to know which parts should be worked first. Bear in mind that small features (such as clouds in a large area of sky, or boats on the sea) should be worked before the surrounding area. It is much easier to work up to and around a small piece of already worked canvas than it is to decide how much space needs to be left for some tiny detail.

Again, if you have put in your cloud and are working the sky round it, always start on a part of the sky where you can work a whole row of your stitch without interruption. It is then easier to work the rows above and below the cloud, so that the two parts join up correctly when they reach the far side.

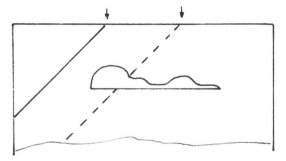

Start the diagonal stitches for the sky around a cloud where a complete row can be worked — ie. from the arrow on the left, not the arrow on the right.

Important features should be stitched in first, and then the less important ones can be worked up to these. For example, if you have drawn a hillside against the sky, the shape of the hill is the important one, so work that first.

Compensation stitches

This is the name given to small stitches which have to be used in areas where there is not room for another whole stitch. The general rule is that as much of the main stitch as possible should be worked, and then the smaller stitch inserted, running in the same direction.

When starting a row where compensation stitches are necessary, it is usually easier to work a part of the row first where a whole stitch will fit in, and then go back to fill in the compensation stitches, rather than try to work out first what is needed. This is particularly the case with rather complex stitches like Milanese or Oriental stitch.

Working on round and oval pictures

It is very difficult when working on round and oval pictures to fit the stitching exactly into the framework drawn on the canvas. This does not matter at all if the picture is going to be mounted and framed, so long as you make sure you have stitched beyond the outline rather than inside it. Always keep a pen or pencil outline of the shape of the original drawing handy to show to the framer.

Stretching the finished canvas

Even such tiny pieces of work as these miniatures, which may not seem out of shape at all, will benefit from this finishing process. Any slight unevenness will be smoothed out and the correct shape of the design and stitches will be assured.

Materials required

piece of fibreboard and ¾ inch (2 cms) tacks
or piece of plywood and a staple gun
LAP starch paste powder (or any good, plain starch paste powder obtainable from DIY or hardware stores)
blunt kitchen knife
a small piece of old towelling
clean damp cloth

Compensation stitches, shown below by dotted lines, are needed in a design where a whole stitch cannot be fitted in the space.

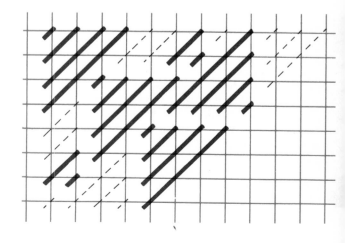

Method

1 On your board, which will be used many times, mark out a grid of squares, about ¼–½ inch (1cm) apart. If there is any possibility that marks may come on to your work from the wood, cover the board with a piece of transparent polythene and fasten down.

2 If the work to be stretched is of a three-dimensional nature, e.g. with French knots or spider's webs in the design, cut a piece of towelling the exact size of your design. This will prevent the raised parts being flattened in the stretching process.

3 Lay the needlepoint face down on the board (with the towelling underneath if it is being used). If the miniature is out of shape, dampen the back of the stitched area with a damp cloth.

4 Line up a set of holes in the canvas about ½ inch (1.2 cms) away from the bottom of your stitching with one of the horizontal grid lines, and fasten down with tacks or staples as you work along, pulling the canvas taut as you go. The staples or tacks should be about ½ inch (1.2 cms) from the stitching.

5 Move to the left-hand side of the needlepoint and, pulling the canvas to the correct size if necessary, line up exactly a set of holes and a vertical grid line. Fasten down as you work up the side of the canvas, again stretching the canvas taut.

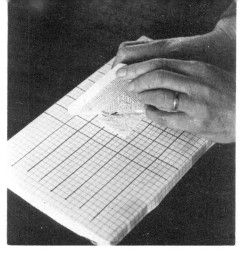
Lay the needlepoint face down on the board, over the towelling.

A staple gun being used to fix the canvas to the board.

6 Repeat at the top and right-hand side of the canvas, possibly dampening the work again slightly to make it easier to pull into shape.

7 Make up a small amount of LAP paste (about 2 teaspoonfuls) to a fluffy, soft consistency and spread thinly but fairly firmly over the design area only, with a blunt knife. Areas where the back of the work is rather bare should have less paste applied and less pressure exerted.

8 Leave to dry naturally.
 This use of paste always gives a most professional finish, and has no adverse effects. If you do not use the paste, you will have to dampen the worked area considerably more when stretching it.

Apply the paste evenly with the blade of a blunt knife to the back of the design.

15

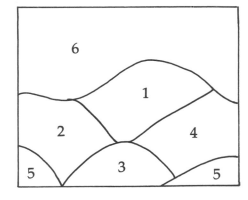

When you have worked on several miniatures of your own design, you will have discovered which are your favourite stitches and may even have made up some new ones to achieve particular effects. This chapter aims to give you a few different ideas on how to give variety to such features as fields, walls, trees and skies which are constant features of landscapes.

Fields

When working a network of fields the landscape is made interesting not only by the use of varied colours, but by the texture and direction of the stitches. Do not use stitches which all slope the same way; vary the angles of slope as well as the direction, use some two-colour stitches and introduce an occasional ploughed field or one full of golden corn. Use some flat stitches and others with a more three-dimensional texture.

Many of the field-effect stitches are shown in the different projects for working, but a few others are introduced here.

1 Sloping field simulated by double twill stitch.

2 Knotted Gobelin stitch field.

3 Ploughed field in single trammed Gobelin.

4 Jacquard stitch field in two colours.

5 Bushes are made of a double French knot background with single French knot flowers.

6 The sky is dramatic in Oriental stitch. Other suitable sky stitches will be found among the projects for working.

The hedges are a mixture of French knots, straight stitches and cross stitches.

Houses

Houses are not the easiest subjects for a beginner, as there is rather a lot of counting of threads before the exact design can be decided upon. This stage is best done on squared paper. Unless the house is the main subject of the miniature, as in 'Country House' (page 47), it will probably be so small that the windows and doors can only be represented by tent stitches. Nevertheless, the exact placing of all the features has to be carefully worked out before starting.

Until the size and placing of the windows has been decided upon it is best not to make the finished dimensions of the house too definite — you might find you had room for only three windows when in fact there were four in your original design. Try out a sample of the window on a spare piece of canvas, so that you know exactly how many strands or holes your chosen stitches cover.

Remember that it is only possible to sew a middle line of any feature along a canvas thread if it has an uneven number of threads altogether — otherwise the middle is a line of holes.

These window panes are outlined in tent stitch, and filled in with a *dark* diagonal satin stitch sloping the opposite way to the tent stitch frame. Note that glass in windows normally looks dark. The bricks are outlined in tent stitch and filled in with a mixture of two shades of brick colour in diagonal satin stitch, sloping the same way.

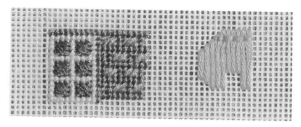

window panes and bricks   **thatch**

Thatch is here simulated by satin stitch, with back stitch along the ridge. The back stitches split the vertical threads to avoid pulling them apart. An extra strand or two can be put into the needle if the long straight stitches do not cover the canvas well enough.

This window frame is tent stitch, with panes of three rows of single trammed Gobelin stitch placed vertically. The dividers are two single stitches, each into the centre hole.
    The wooden weather-boarding is Gobelin stitches over 3 horizontal threads.

window and weather-boarding

leaded lights with pebble-dash

These diamond-paned leaded windows are lattice stitch filled in with three diagonal satin stitches.
    The pebble-dashing alongside is tiny random French knots, worked with three strands only, in two shades of grey.

Weaving stitch can be used for roofs or walls. Here the roof has been given ridge tiles of single trammed Gobelin stitch.

To simulate a tiled roof with moss and lichen on it, a single strand of green has been added to the tile-coloured embroidery thread. The stitch for the tiles is single brick, and the ridge tiles are Gobelin stitches over 2 horizontals.

Random diagonal satin stitch blocks make a realistic looking stone wall, or paving.

designs for roofs

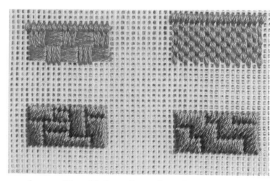

random satin stitch and random Byzantine stitch

Random Byzantine stitch, with irregular steps, makes an interesting wall, or paving.

Trees

Trees come in a bewildering variety of shapes and sizes, and this richness must be shown in the needlepoint by using many different stitches. The examples below are by no means comprehensive, and you have plenty of scope for your own ideas.

Trees of any size can be made from interlocking **leaf stitch** (see diagram 6a in 'Sheep in a landscape', page 23). The trees do not have to be triangular; they can be built out in any direction and half stitches can be used. Trunk: horizontal satin stitch with a tramming thread underneath.

fir tree

leaf stitch tree

Fir tree

This tree is made from single leaf stitches placed underneath each other. Fir cones made from French knots have been placed where the stitches meet. Leaf stitches can be graduated in size to make a more pointed tree, as in 'Inca's television' (see page 36). Trunk: cross stitches over 2 threads with a tramming thread underneath.

18

Fruit tree

Trees of any shape, with varying colours of fruits or flowers, are easily and effectively made with French knots. Trunk: single cross stitch, over one intersection of the canvas.

Pine tree

Cross stitches over one intersection of the canvas make a very dense cover which, because it is such a small stitch, is very suitable for the odd shapes of Scots Pines. Trunk: tent stitch.

fruit tree   pine tree

a A beautiful ring shape is made by interlocking four graduated sheaf stitches at right angles. The middle should be filled in with basketweave tent stitches for maximum effect. Trunk: back stitches over 4 threads.

b Here the graduated sheaf stitches have been placed sideways underneath each other. They are interlocked at either end. A smaller version of the stitch over 2, 4, 6, 4 and 2 threads can be used to achieve the required shape. Fill in between sheaf stitches with tent stitch. Trunk: four double cross stitches.

c Small-size graduated sheaf stitches over 2, 4, 6, 4, 2 threads have been worked vertically and placed underneath each other. French knot fir cones are placed at the joining of the sheaf stitches. Trunk: one long stitch over an *uneven* number of threads, 'tied' in the middle by a thread taken up and down through the middle hole covered by the stitch.

d Graduated sheaf stitches are here made into a larger tree. Trunk: a single long stitch over an *uneven* number of threads, 'tied' in the middle as in the tree above.

A **spider's web stitch** is here worked over a radius of 6 threads, and French knots placed round the edge between each of the spokes. Trunk: French knots placed in a vertical line.

Small **upright crosses** over 2 threads make a very firm knobbly surface. Any shape can be made, as with the ordinary single cross stitch. Trunk: upright cross stitch.

spider's web stitch   upright crosses

5 SOURCES OF INSPIRATION AND REFERENCE

One of the main difficulties for the inexperienced in any sort of craftwork is knowing what to make. In needlepoint a great deal of time can be spent in learning all the wonderful stitches, but they are of little use unless they can be used effectively in actual projects.

Sources of inspiration are all around us — the difficulty lies in training our eyes and mind to realize the possibilities in what we see. The natural world can inspire many different types of project and as with several of the examples in the book, real or imaginary landscapes may be stylized to a certain extent so they can be satisfactorily portrayed in needlepoint. Subjects for abstracts too are often found in natural forms, trees, flowers, fungi or stones can make pleasing colour and shape patterns which may look stunning when translated into stitchery. The needlework of past ages is also a fascinating study, and although few people would want to copy

slavishly the masterpieces of previous centuries, nevertheless it gives one a sense of continuity to take a design worked perhaps in the sixteenth century and use it as the basis for a modern needlepoint embroidery incorporating stitches which were unknown at the time of the original piece of work. Such a piece is the elephant in Chapter 16.

Needlepoint scrap book

The basis for this is just an ordinary scrap book into which you paste everything you come across which seems as though it might be useful, now or at some time in the future, in the making of a design. Especially useful sources for miniatures are Christmas and birthday cards, and post cards purchased at stately homes or museums. Even advertisements are of interest, especially those from glossy magazines, as are photographs you and other people have taken, sketches you have made when something caught your eye . . . and so on. The list is really endless and the making of the scrap book tends to become something of an end in itself. Just looking through this book may give you an idea for a new project, which perhaps is only very loosely based on any particular picture. We all need to be bombarded with ideas to get our imaginations working.

Stitch dictionary

As you learn new stitches, it is a good idea to make a diagram and sample of each one and add them to a stitch dictionary. Besides being an interesting and attractive collection in its own right, it is useful when deciding what stitches are most suitable for the job in hand, and as none of the reference books lists all the possible stitches it is invaluable for those times when you cannot quite remember how you did a certain stitch.

To make a stitch dictionary you need an A4 size loose-leaf binder with a set of transparent pockets, and a pad of ¼ inch (6 mm) or larger squared paper. For each stitch make a diagram similar to the ones in this book, if necessary numbering where the needle goes in and out. Alongside the diagram stick in a small piece of canvas with the stitch worked on it, in

different colourways if it is a two- or three-colour stitch. You can also make a note of your own thoughts about the stitch; for example, where it seems to be especially useful, or what sort of colours suit it best, whether it covers the canvas well or otherwise.

In no time this becomes a document which your friends will find fascinating, and eventually you will be adding stitches you have invented yourself. The stitches may be worked in any thread on whatever canvas you choose.

6 SHEEP IN A LANDSCAPE

This is a good picture to work first, as it is extremely simple in design, with large areas of the same stitch. Only a few colours are used and detail is kept to a minimum, but the inclusion of the barn and three sheep makes the landscape come alive.

Materials

18s mono interlock canvas 4½ x 5½ inches (11.5 x 14 cm)
Madeira 6-strand embroidery cottons, one pack of each colour, numbers as follows:

sky: grey blue, M932
sheep and cloud: White
fields, trees and grassy hummocks in foreground: dark and light greens, M369, M3052, M520
barn: light brown, M640
roof: brick brown, M356
tree trunks, windows, chimney and heads of sheep: dark brown, M898

If you are using a different make of embroidery cotton, match up the colours on the picture.

Method and order of working

1 Bind the canvas with masking tape.

2 Lay the canvas over the drawing of 'Sheep in a landscape' and trace the design on to the canvas, using an HB pencil or pale-coloured, waterproof fibre-tipped pen.

3 Work the *trees* first. The large tree is four interlocking leaf stitches (see diagram 6a) in M520, and the small tree is just one leaf stitch. The trunks are satin stitch worked across 2 vertical threads. Be sure to work the satin stitches in an 'over and over' fashion, as shown by the numbers in diagram 6a, or else they will not lie parallel.

4 *Foreground* these humps, representing bushes, are worked in the three colours of green in vertical satin stitch. Keep the tension even.

5 *Left-hand field* single trammed Gobelin stitch (M3052). You will need to use a half-size compensation stitch at several points to make the line of the hillside smooth. The *sheep* are worked in White, the heads in brown (M898). Each sheep is incorporated into a different row of the single trammed Gobelin stitch. When a sheep row is reached, work the sheep first, with its own small tramming thread as on diagram 6b. The rest of the row is then worked, the tramming thread being taken down behind the sheep and out again on the other side.

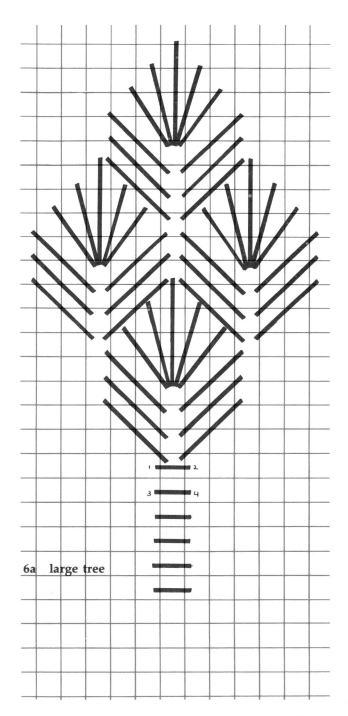

6a   large tree

23

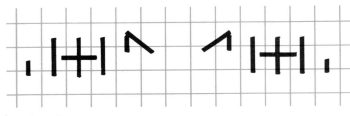

6b   sheep

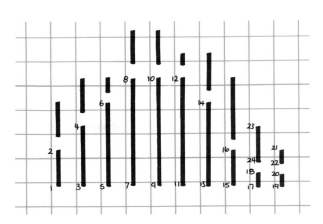

6c   two-layer cloud

6. *Barn*: the roof is worked in single brick stitch (M356). The ends of the gable consist of single, long, sloping stitches. The window is two straight stitches worked horizontally across 2 threads (M898). The walls are in satin stitch (M640). Stitches are worked vertically on the gable and horizontally on the walls, divided at the corner so that a line shows to form the corner of the building. The chimney is two small satin stitches worked vertically over 2 threads (M898).

7. *Right-hand field*: Parisian stitch used sideways (M369). Quite a few compensation stitches must be used at the sky end of the rows to achieve a smooth edge to the field.

8. *Clouds*: upright satin stitches in White, varying in height from over one thread to over 6 threads. The effect is enhanced by working the clouds in two 'layers' (diagram 6c) to give the look of banked-up clouds. The satin stitch must again be worked 'over and over' — no cutting across the top at the back to save on cotton, it's not worth it.

9. *Sky*: diagonal mosaic stitch (M932). Start from the left, where you can work several rows before having to divide the row round the clouds.

10. *Finishing*: follow the instructions in Chapter 3. When dry, have the miniature professionally mounted and framed, unless you are very skilled yourself. Make certain that the framer has equipment to cut oval mounts satisfactorily before leaving your work with him.

24

The idea for this miniature came from a watercolour on a greetings card (see page 28). The whole mood of the scene could be changed by altering the colours of the sky.

Materials

18s mono interlock canvas 4½ x 5½ inches (11.5 x 14 cm)
Madeira 6-strand embroidery cottons, one pack of each colour, numbers as follows:

> *sky*: grey blue, M775, M932
> *trees and bushes*: green, M319, dark green, M500, brown, M938
> *large mountain*: heather, M3041 mixed with grey, M317
> *small mountain*: mauve, M3042 mixed with dark grey, M318
> *grass*: green, M367
> *sheep*: White, brown, M938
> *water*: blues, M932, M827, M813, M930, M931, M926
> *marshy area*: olive green, M3012

If you are using a different make of embroidery cotton, match up the colours in the picture.

Method and order of working

1 Bind the canvas with masking tape.

2 Lay the canvas over the drawing of 'Lake scene' and trace the design on to the canvas, using an HB pencil or pale-coloured, waterproof fibre-tipped pen.

3 Work the **trees on the right** first. The centre tree is the darker green (M500). The treetop shapes are filled in with single cross stitch

over one intersection of the canvas. Trunks are tent stitches (M938).

4 *Larger mountain* Oblique Slav stitch, with a mixture of three strands of M3041 and three of M317. It is rather tricky to keep the pattern correct between the trees, but at least give the stitches the right upward slant, otherwise it may look odd.

5 *Smaller mountain* twill stitch over 3 threads, in a mixture of three strands of M3042 and three of M318.

6 *Sky* can now be filled in. Cashmere stitch is used, in two colours of blue (M775 and M932), which looks when finished as though it is sheeting down with rain — rather appropriate! Do not worry if you find this quite a difficult stitch, though it looks simple. Everyone seems to have trouble with it, but the effect makes it worthwhile.

7 *Grass* texture is given to the grassy bank under the trees by the use of single trammed Gobelin stitch in M367. (Do not forget to include the sheep — see below).

8 *Sheep* put into the second and third line down, as you work the grass. They may follow the design in 'Sheep in a landscape', or can have white French knots for their bodies instead.

9 *Bushes* the larger bush is worked in M500 in single cross stitch, the same as the trees, while the smaller bush is made up of four French knots.

10 *Marshy area and water* both worked in random long and short satin stitch. This must *not* be worked as though you were darning, i.e. in and out along a line of holes (as below).

This is because when working the spaces in between, you split the thread each time and the general effect is very untidy.

Instead, you have to work down random diagonals, so that the thread is always drawn back under the stitch you have worked, leaving the hole open for the adjoining stitch, as in diagram 7b.

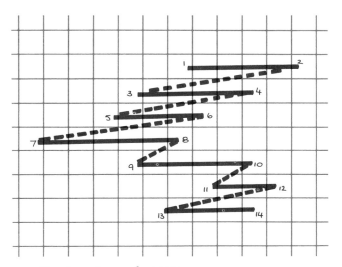

7b   how to work water

This results in a lot of long threads being carried across the back of the work, but it is the effect on the front which is more important.

The *Marshy area* is worked in M3012 in long and short satin stitch, as described above.

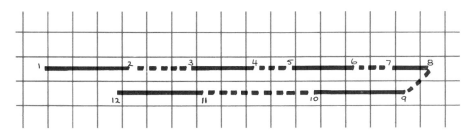

7a   how not to work water

27

A watercolour by Trudi Finch.

The *lake* itself is worked in the blues indicated above, in long and short satin stitch as previously described. Use a mixture of the paler shades under the mountains, the darker shades in the right foreground to represent shadow from the trees, and the middle range colours in the left foreground.

Finishing follow the instructions in Chapter 3. When dry, have the miniature professionally mounted and framed unless you are very skilled yourself. Cutting oval openings in mounts is a specialized job.

THATCHED COTTAGE

A depiction of a traditional thatched cottage with a rambler rose growing round the windows, and sheep resting on the hillside behind.

Materials

18s mono interlock canvas 4½ x 5½ inches (11.5 x 14 cm)
Madeira 6-strand embroidery cottons, one pack of each colour, numbers as follows:

sky: blue, M926
cloud and sheep: White
trees, hillside, lawn and hummocks in foreground: greens, M3052, M369, M520
fence, window and door frames, tree trunks and heads of sheep: dark brown, M898
door, windows and smoke: dark grey, M317
thatch: ochre, M783
cottage wall: Ecru
path and chimney: stone, M3032
rose bush: dark green, M520
flowers: pink, M602

If using a different make of embroidery cotton, match up the colours on the picture.

Method and order of working

1 Bind the canvas with masking tape.

2 Lay the canvas over the drawing of 'Thatched cottage' and trace the design on to the canvas, using an HB pencil or pale-coloured, waterproof fibre-tipped pen.

3 The **thatched roof** is worked first (M783), using long and short satin stitch, following the diagram. Work the left-hand half of the roof as a mirror image of the right-hand half shown on diagram 8a. All the thatch is the same colour.

4 **Chimney** three straight stitches (M3032) over 5 horizontal threads.

5 **Windows and door** work frames in tent stitch (M898) as on diagram 8b, and fill in with upright straight stitches (M317).

6 **Small tree** three Hungarian stitches on top of each other (M3052), with French knot flowers worked in three strands of M602 placed at random. The trunk is a single vertical stitch (M898).

7 **Cottage wall** brick stitch worked sideways over 4 threads of canvas in Ecru.

8 **Rose bush** work branches of rose bush in back stitch (M520), three strands only. Place

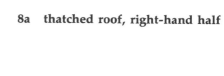

8a thatched roof, right-hand half

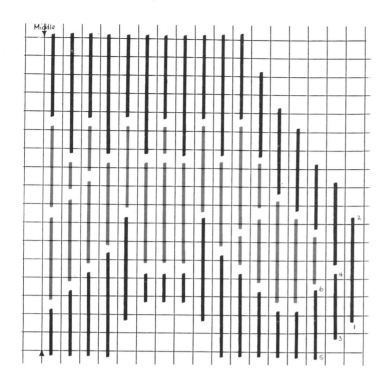

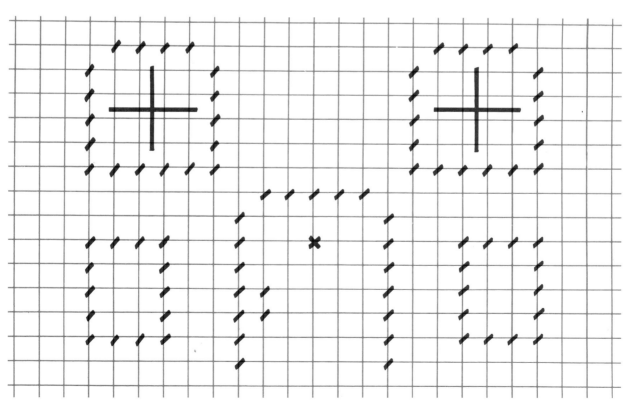

8b windows and door

31

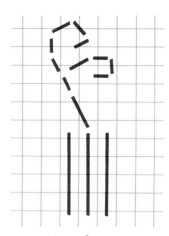

8c   chimney and smoke

roses at random, making French knots with three strands of M602.

9 *Sky* twill stitch over 3 canvas threads, the pattern running from top left to bottom right (M926).

10 *Cloud* with White, work a few short rows of darning stitches in and out of the twill stitch to represent the cloud.

11 *Smoke* using back stitch (M317), work two curls of smoke as on diagram 8c, noting that the canvas will not be visible.

12 *Large tree* interlocking leaf stitches (M520). Follow diagram 8d.
The trunk is a narrow band of brick stitch over 4 canvas threads (M898).

13 *Hillside* diagonal ground stitch (M3052), the diagonal running from top right to bottom left. Insert the sheep as you come to them (White and M898), following diagram 8e.

14 *Fence* work back stitches (M898) to represent the lattice fence.

15 *Hummocks* in the foreground: vertical satin stitch (M520 and M3052).

16 *Path* single cross stitch (M3032), over one intersection of the canvas.

17 *Lawn* single trammed Gobelin stitch (M369).

18 *Finishing* follow the instructions in Chapter 3. When dry, have the miniature professionally mounted and framed unless you are very skilled yourself. Make certain that the framer has equipment to cut oval mounts satisfactorily before leaving your work with him.

8d   large tree

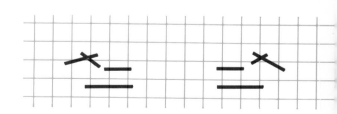

8e   sheep

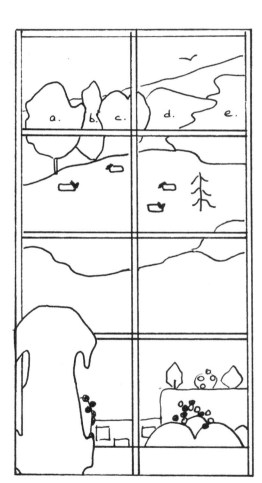

Inca, the author's dog, a Hungarian Vizsla, is a delightful character. At breakfast time she sits glued to the view of wildlife in the garden outside, hence 'Inca's television'.

Materials

18s mono interlock canvas 6½ x 4½ inches (16.5 x 11.5 cm)
Madeira 6-strand embroidery cottons, one pack of each colour, numbers as follows:
  sky: blue, M932
  background, wall and path: light brown, M640
  trees and bushes: blue-greens, M500, M501, M503, M367
  lawns: green, M368
  sheep: White
  dog, tree trunk: brown, M898
  flowers: pink, M962, yellow, M445
  door frame, sheeps' heads and buzzard: dark brown, M3371
If you are using a different make of embroidery cotton, match up the colours on the picture.

Method and order of working

1 Bind the canvas with masking tape.

2 Lay the canvas over the drawing of 'Inca's television' and trace the design on to the canvas, using an HB pencil or pale-coloured, waterproof fibre-tipped pen.

3 Work the *dog* first, using basketweave tent stitch (M898). Follow diagram 9a.

4 *Door frame* work as far as possible in basketweave tent stitch (M3371). Using the diagonal stitch will prevent the work from pulling out of shape. There are three rows of

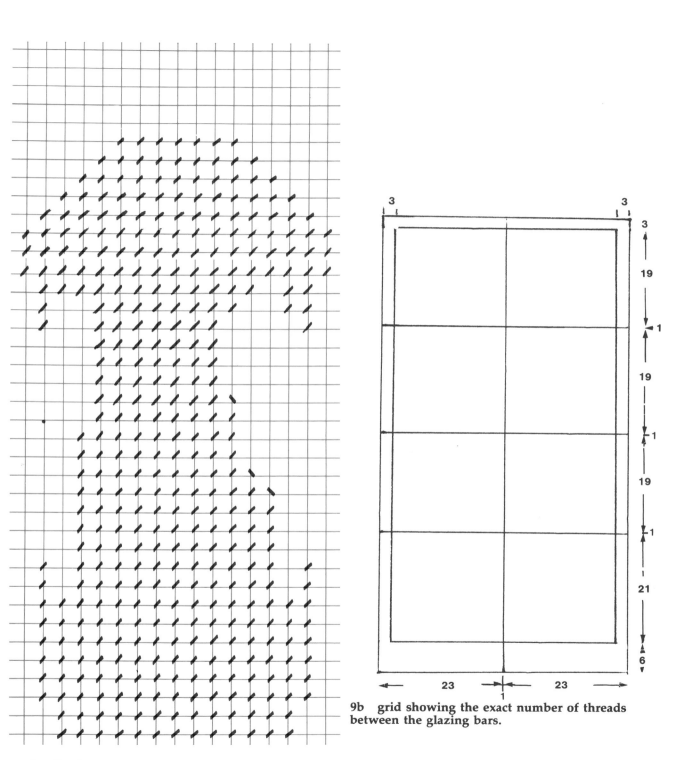

9a the dog

9b grid showing the exact number of threads between the glazing bars.

35

M3371 along the top of the frame, three rows down each side and six rows along the bottom. The dividers between the glass panes are each one row of M3371.

Diagram 9b gives the exact number of threads in each section of the frame.

5 *Trees* from the left (see diagram, page 34) the trees are worked as follows:

   a Single brick stitch (M503). Trunk, one straight stitch (M898).

   b Three leaf stitches (M501), the bottom one wider than the other two.

   c Hungarian stitch 1, over 1, 3, 5, 3 threads (M367).

   d Small Parisian stitch, over 1 and 3 threads (M500)

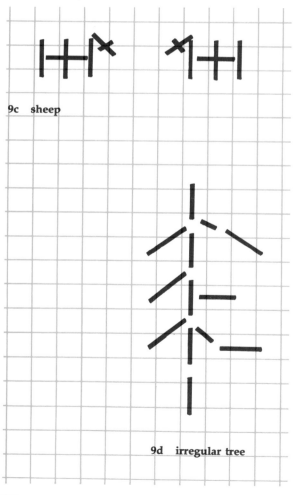

9c sheep

9d irregular tree

   e Graduated sheaf stitch, over 2, 4, 6, 4, 2 threads, worked sideways and interlocked (M367 and M503 mixed: three strands of each). See Stitch directory.

6 *Background* (behind the trees) single brick stitch (M640).

7 *Sky* diagonal mosaic stitch, running from top left to bottom right (M932). The buzzard is two small straight stitches (M3371), worked on top of the mosaic stitch.

8 *Rear lawn* single trammed Gobelin stitch (M368). Add the *sheep* as you come to them, White bodies, brown heads (M3371). Each sheep is incorporated into a different row of the single trammed Gobelin stitch. When a sheep row is reached, work the sheep first, with its own small tramming thread as on diagram 9c. The rest of the row is then worked, the tramming thread being taken down behind the sheep and out again on the other side.

9 *Tree on the rear lawn* work as surface stitchery on top of Gobelin stitch, using back stitch (M501).

10 *Bush on the right* random vertical satin stitches (M367).

11 *Lawn* Hungarian stitch 2 (M368).

12 *Hummocks in the foreground* vertical satin stitch (M503).

13 *Wall* Parisian stitch sideways over 3 and 1 threads (M640).

14 *Path* diagonal ground stitch, with tent stitch between the rows (M640).

15 *Bushes growing in the wall* a variety of stitch motifs including leaf, French knots and Hungarian stitch 1.

16 *Flowers* place randomly, using three strands each of M962 and M445.

17 *Finishing* follow the instructions in Chapter 3. When dry, have the miniature professionally mounted and framed unless you are very skilled yourself.

The outside row of the door frame all the way round will be covered by the mount.

10 ROCKY COAST

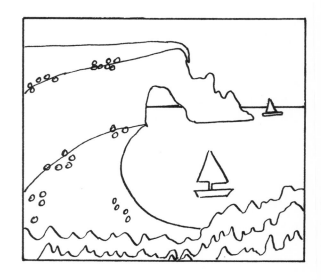

This scene was inspired by memories of the magnificent cliff arch of Durdle Door on the coast of Dorset.

Materials

18s mono interlock canvas 4½ inches (11.5 cm) square
Madeira 6-strand embroidery cottons, one pack of each colour, numbers as follows:

cliff face: browns, M840, M640
cliff top: greens, M367, M890
sand: ochre, M834
sea: blues, M926, M927, M930, M932
boats: M938, White
sky: pale blue, M775
foreground: browns, M938, M640, M840
flowers: rose, M223
boulders: light brown, M640

If using a different make of embroidery cotton, match up the colours on the picture.

Method and order of working

1 Bind the canvas with masking tape.

2 Lay the canvas over the drawing of 'Dorset coast' and trace the design on to the canvas, using an HB pencil or pale-coloured, waterproof fibre-tipped pen.

3 Work the *cliff face* first, in double twill stitch. The longer vertical stitches are over 3 canvas threads and are worked with nine strands of M840. The shorter stitches are over 2 canvas threads (M640), and are worked with the normal 6-strand cotton without extra threads, thus giving the cliff face a rugged texture.

4 *Cliff top* single brick stitch worked sideways in M367. Along the very top, and taken one stitch down the end of the cliff, is a row of back stitches over 4 threads in M890.

5 *Sky* diagonal ground stitch in M775.

6 *Sand* Hungarian stitch 2, worked sideways in M834.

7 *Sailing boats* worked in M938 (hull), and White (sail). Follow the diagrams below.

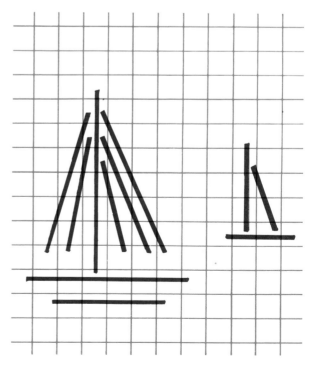

10a and 10b the designs for the sailing boats

8 *Sea* random long and short satin stitch (see instruction 10 in 'Lake scene'), in all the blues except M775. If your stitches have a tendency not to cover very well with this stitch, it is a good idea to colour the canvas before stitching (see page 10) or to put an extra couple of strands of cotton in your needle.

9 *Foreground* random Florentine stitch in M938, M640 and M840.

10 *Pink flowers on the cliff top* small French knots made with three strands of M223.

11 *Boulders on the sand* randomly placed French knots in M640.

12 *Finishing* follow the instructions in Chapter 3. When dry, have the miniature professionally mounted and framed unless you are very skilled yourself.

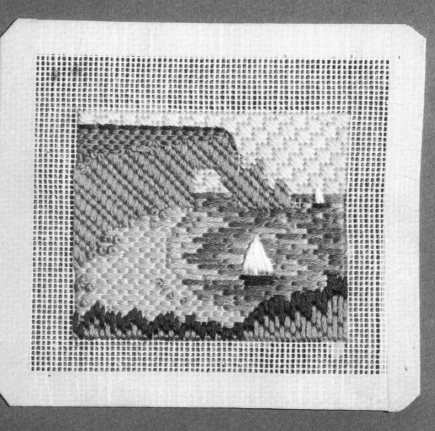

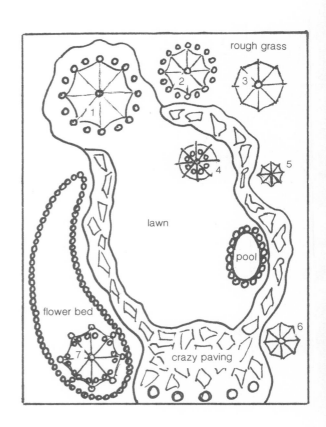

As its name implies, the inspiration for this design was a plan for a garden.

Materials, and sizes of spider's web stitches

18s mono interlock canvas 4½ x 5½ inches (11.5 x 14 cm)
Madeira 6-strand embroidery cottons, one pack of each colour, numbers as follows:

lawn: pale green, M369
rough grass: green, M368
trees and bushes: (spider's web stitches, see diagram 11a)

1 M501. French knots M3350 and M962. Radius 8 canvas threads (only 6 over diagonals).

2 M503. French knots M501 and M369. Radius 5 canvas threads (4 over diagonals).

3 M500. Outer two rings M501. French knot M369. Radius 6 threads (5 over diagonals).

4 M503 (centre 3 rings) and M501. French knots M3350. Radius 5 threads (4 over diagonals).

5 M962. Outer ring M501. Radius 4 threads (3 over diagonals).

6 M3350. French knot M501. Radius 4 threads (3 over diagonals).

7 M725. French knots M501 and M725. Radius 6 threads (5 over diagonals).

pool: blue M311. French knots M3354 and M3350. Size: 10 canvas threads high, and 7 wide.

crazy paving path and patio: fawn M840 and M644.

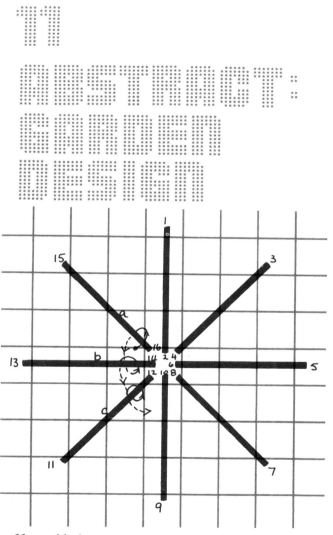

11a   spider's web stitch

43

bushes on patio: double French knots
　　(twice round needle) dark green, M500
flowers in bottom right-hand corner and up
　　right-hand side: yellow, M445, pink,
　　M3354, yellow, M725
flowers in flower bed: random mixture of
　　all the colours

If you are using a different make of
embroidery cotton, match up the colours on
the picture.

Method and order of working

1 Bind the canvas with masking tape.

2 Lay the canvas over the drawing of 'Garden
design' and trace the design on to the canvas,
using an HB pencil or pale-coloured,
waterproof fibre-tipped pen.

3 Work the **trees and bushes** first, in spider's
web stitch and French knots in the colours
and sizes indicated above, and as on the
picture.

4 **Crazy paving path and patio** tent stitch
(M840), leaving irregularly shaped spaces to
be filled in with satin stitch (M644). The path
round the tree at the top left is tent stitch only.

5 **Bushes on patio** five double French knots
(M500) at the back of the patio represent
small shrubs in pots — possibly bay trees.

6 **Flower bed** outline in French knots (M501),
and fill in with random French knots in all the
available colours (do not do too many green
knots).

7 **Pool**·colour the area of the pool with blue
felt tip (permanent), and work over with M311
in satin stitch. This gives a more solid colour.
Outline with French knots, alternately M3354
and M3350.

8 **Lawn** Hungarian stitch 2 (M369).

9 **Flowers** work a few flowers up the right-
hand side of the patio and path in French
knots (M445, M3354 and M725).

10 **Rough grass area** single brick stitch (M368)

11 **Finishing** follow the instructions in Chapter
3. When dry, have the miniature professionally
mounted and framed unless you are very
skilled yourself.

12 COUNTRY HOUSE

This miniature is worked in just one colour, thus the design only shows up because of the different shapes, textures and directional qualities of the stitches. The colour used here is ecru, but another colour could be chosen. Do not use a dark colour, however, as the stitches would then not catch the light so well and the outlines would be less distinct.

Materials

18s mono interlock canvas 6 x 4½ inches (15 x 11.5 cm)
Madeira 6-strand embroidery cotton: Ecru, or alternative make of embroidery cotton. You will need three packs.

Method and order of working

1 Bind the canvas with masking tape.

2 Lay the canvas over the drawing of 'Country house' and trace the design on to the canvas, using an HB pencil or *pale-coloured*, waterproof fibre-tipped pen. It is especially important that the drawing should be pale, as all the stitching is in a light colour and any dark lines will show through. Make sure that the top of the roof of the house lies along a horizontal thread of the canvas. All other horizontals should then also be along threads. The canvas should be laid with the selvedges at the top or bottom of the picture. You will find that the canvas 'squares' are then very slightly taller than they are broad.

3 Work the *tree on the left* first, in interlocking leaf stitch. The trunk is horizontal satin stitch. See instructions in 'Sheep in a landscape' page 23.

4 *Roof* single brick stitch. As you come to the chimney, work this in Small Parisian stitch sideways, with the side of the chimney in diagonal satin stitch.
   The roof of the extension should be worked after that of the main house, so that the stitches do not line up with those of the rest of the house.
   A diagram is given overleaf for the windows and doors of the house.

5 *Windows* outlined in tent stitch, and filled in with diagonal satin stitches running the opposite way from the tent stitch edging.

6 *Front door* outlined in horizontal and diagonal satin stitches, and the door itself is worked in twill stitch over 3 threads. A single straight stitch marks the handle.

7 The *rounded-topped door* of the extension is worked in twill stitch over 3 threads, and outlined by four straight stitches.

8 *Walls of the house and extension* single brick stitch placed sideways. The foliage at the bottom left of the house should be worked at this stage as a series of low hummocks to the left of the front door in vertical satin stitch.

9 *Tree on the right* interlocking graduated sheaf stitches, worked sideways and placed under one another, with double French knots (two twists round the needle) filling the holes in between them. See stitch directory.

The tree trunk is two vertical rows of double cross stitch over 2 threads.

10 *Sky* Milanese stitch worked from top right to bottom left.

11 *Bushes on the right in front of the house* two spider's web stitches are worked over 6 threads, and one over 8 threads (i.e. 3 and 4 threads out from the centres).

The hummocky area is worked in varying lengths of vertical satin stitch, and above them is an area of single French knots.

12 *Background between the bushes and the tree* mosaic stitch.

13 *Foreground* the left front is a small area of vertical satin stitch representing bushes; otherwise the whole area is worked in Hungarian stitch 2.

14 *Finishing* follow the instructions in Chapter 3. When dry, have the miniature professionally mounted and framed unless you are very skilled yourself.

12a   the windows and doors of the house

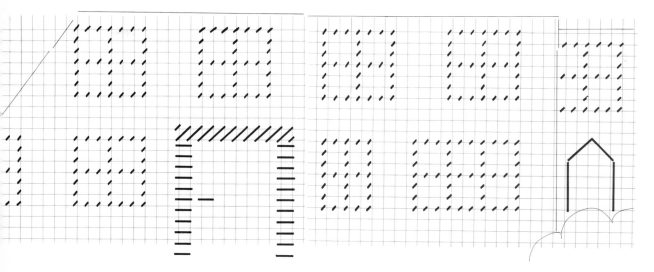

13 WINTER EVENING

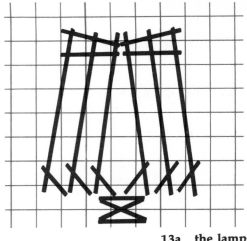

13a   the lamp

This is an interior design in warm colours, giving the impression of a snug winter evening in front of the fire, with the pets in the warmest spot, as usual! The inspiration for this was an advertisement for fireplaces in a magazine. This is probably the most complicated of the designs to execute, as there is greater detail than in the others.

Materials

18s mono interlock canvas 5 x 5¾ inches (13 x 14.5 cm)
Madeira 6-strand embroidery cottons, one pack of each colour, numbers as follows:

> *wall (upper part)*: Ecru
> *wall (lower part)*: ochre, M834
> *picture frames*: dark brown, M3371
> *mantelpiece*: rust, M975
> *fireplace surround and picture mounts*:
>   fawn, M644
> *fireback*: slate, M317
> *pictures*: slate, M317 and green, M367
> *fire*: dark and light orange, M720, M722,
>   slate, M317, yellow, M725
> *grate bars, cat, clock hands and dog collar*:
>   Black
> *log basket*: fawn, M642, dark brown, M898
> *carpet*: greens, M368, M369
> *dog*: dark brown, M898
> *clock, candlestick and lamp base*: golden,
>   M783
> *candle*: wine red, M815
> *clock dial*: White
> *lampshade*: greens, M368, M367

If you are using a different make of embroidery cotton, match up the colours on the picture.

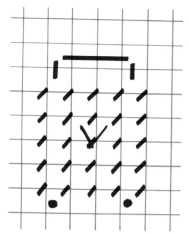

13b   the clock

Method and order of working

1 Bind the canvas with masking tape.

2 Lay the canvas over the drawing of 'Winter evening' and trace the design on to the canvas, using an HB pencil or pale-coloured, waterproof fibre-tipped pen.

3 Work the *picture frames* first, in tent stitch with M3371.

4 *Upper part of wall* Hungarian stitch 2, in Ecru. Work down as far as the top of the lamp, clock and candle. Add these features and the mantelpiece before finishing the upper wall.

5 *Lampshade* work 6 straight stitches (M368), with small stitches at top and bottom as shown in diagram 13a. (M367).

6 *Lamp base* four stitches (M783), as shown in diagram 13a.

7 *Clock* work the case in tent stitch (M783). The feet are two French knots, and the handle three straight stitches. See diagram 13b.

   The dial is tent stitch in White. The hands are two short stitches in black (2 strands) on top of the tent stitches.

8 *Candlestick* straight stitches (M783) as shown in diagram 13c. The candle is one straight stitch (M815).

9 *Mantelpiece* M975, using diagram 13d as a guide. This shows the top right-hand corner.

   Work the top of the mantelpiece, and then, before completely working the sides, put in the dog and the log basket with logs.

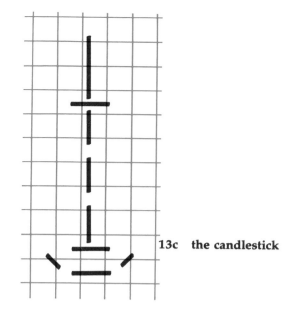

13c   the candlestick

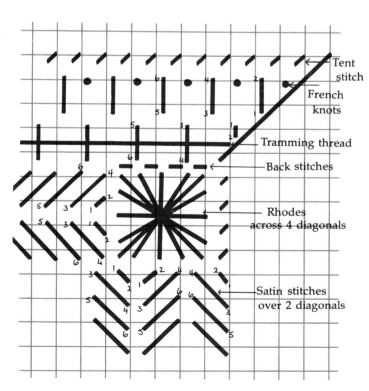

Tent stitch

French knots

Tramming thread

Back stitches

Rhodes across 4 diagonals

Satin stitches over 2 diagonals

13d   a corner of the mantelpiece

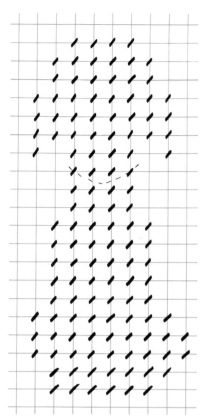

13e   the dog

10 *Dog* tent stitch (M898), as in diagram 13e. The collar is two straight surface stitches (Black).

11 *Log basket* a small weaving-stitch over 3 threads (M642). When finished, thread the needle with 2 strands of M898 and go over the right-hand stitch of each group of three upright stitches, to give a three-dimensional effect. *Logs* horizontal satin stitch (M898), outlined on top and left-hand side with M642.

12 Finish sides of mantelpiece.

13 Finish upper wall. The dividing line between the upper and lower wall is a line of single trammed Gobelin in Ecru.

14 *Lower part of wall* Hungarian stitch 2 (M834).

15 *Cat* work the ears first, outlining each with two straight stitches (Black). The rest of the cat shape is filled in with randomly placed French knots in Black. The tail is worked in back stitches.

16 *Carpet* Small Parisian stitch placed sideways. The long stitches over 3 threads of canvas are in M368, and the short stitches over 1 thread are in M369.

17 *Fire surround* inside the mantelpiece, work in upright single brick stitch (M644). Below the fire, work single brick stitch sideways (M644).

18 *Fire* work as diagram 13f (M720, M722, M317 and M725).

19 *Grate bars* Black back stitches. Insert a few small stitches of fire colours in between the bars.

20 *Fireback* tent stitch (M317).

21 *Pictures* work the mounts in tent stitch (M644), 2 rows all round in lower pictures, and 1 row in upper pictures. The subjects of the pictures are fairly random satin and tent stitches to suggest landscapes. The bottom right picture is the author's sheep 'trade mark', in White French knots for the body, brown (M898) for the head.

22 *Finishing* follow the instructions in Chapter 3. When dry, have the miniature professionally mounted and framed unless you are very skilled yourself.

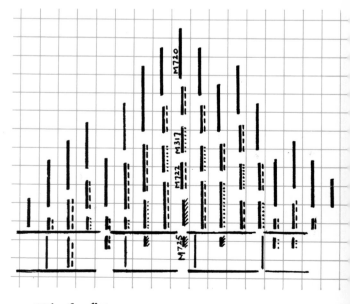

13f   the fire

53

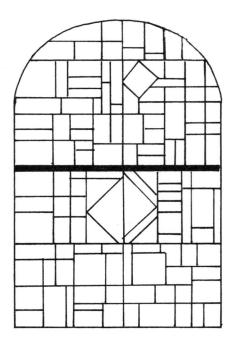

The original idea for this design came from a small window in the chapel dedicated to St Michael, on top of one of the volcanic puys at Le Puy in France. One has to climb hundreds of rather slippery steps to reach the top, so plenty of time is taken to admire the view and the simple chapel.

The colours of the window are depicted entirely in satin stitch, which catches the light well, giving the idea of glass.

Materials

18s mono interlock canvas 5½ x 4½ inches (14 x 11.5 cm)
Madeira 6-strand embroidery cottons, one pack of each colour, numbers as follows:

Black
White
Red: M349
Dark green: M890
Pale green: M369
Turquoise green: M943
Dark blue: M824
Pale blue: M932
Pink: M963
Dark yellow: M725
Pale yellow: M3078

If you are using a different make of embroidery cotton, match up the colours on the picture.

Method and order of working

1 Bind the canvas with masking tape.

2 Lay the canvas over the drawing of 'Stained glass window' and trace the design on to the canvas, using a black, fine-line, waterproof fibre-tipped marker. Make sure the heavy horizontal line across the middle lies exactly along a thread. There are 39 vertical threads between the outside rows of back stitches at the base of the design.

3 Work the divisions between the sections and round the edge of the window in back stitch over one canvas thread. Do not worry if your divisions are not exactly the same size as those on the model.

   The back stitches round the arched top of the picture will have to be over more than one thread to follow the shape exactly.

4 Work the horizontal line across the middle in single cross stitch.

5 With appropriately coloured waterproof felt-tipped markers, shade carefully the areas to be covered by the dark threads, i.e. the dark blue, dark green, turquoise and red. If suitable felt-tips are not available use coloured pencils.

6 Following diagram 14a, fill in the areas with the different colours using satin stitch. The arrows show whether the stitch should lie vertically or horizontally, and the number indicates the number of stitches in each section. The stitches for the glass use the same holes as are used for the back stitch edgings. Keep untwisting the thread so that the stitches lie flat.

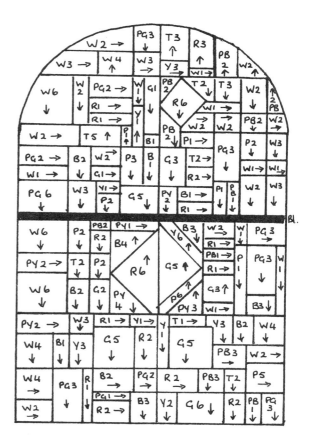

14a diagram to show the colour, number and direction of the stitches

Bl	Black	**B**	Dark blue
W	White	**PB**	Pale blue
R	Red	**P**	Pink
G	Dark green	**Y**	Dark yellow
PG	Pale green	**PY**	Pale yellow
T	Turquoise green		

55

7 When completed, to facilitate mounting, colour a narrow band around the work in black, and work a row of black back-stitches round the entire window. These back-stitches may be over 3 or 4 threads, and should be covered by the mount.

8 *Finishing* follow the instructions in Chapter 3. When dry, have the miniature professionally mounted and framed unless you are very skilled yourself.

The original stained glass window

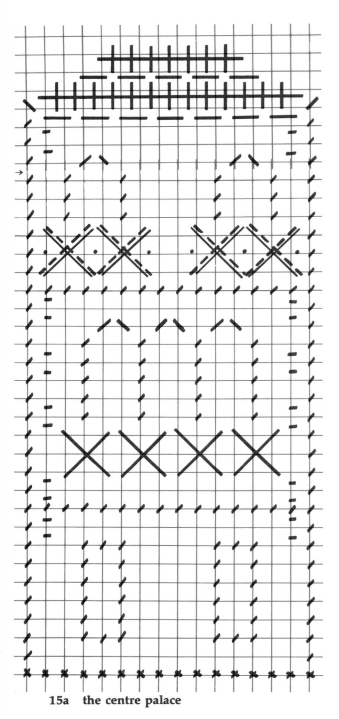

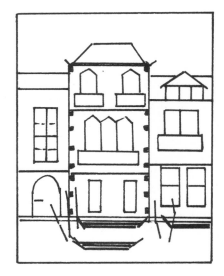

15 VENICE

Amid the wonders of Venice this little palazzo stood out from all the others on the Grand Canal — they were vast and crumbling, whereas this small one had recently been cleaned and repaired and seemed a tiny jewel.

Materials

18s mono interlock canvas 4½ × 4 inches (11.5 × 10 cm)
Madeira 6-strand embroidery cottons, one pack of each colour, numbers as follows:

sky: grey blue, M927
palaces: Ecru, fawn, M642, brick, M356, terracotta, M762, stone, M407, slate grey, M317
canal: blue grey, M930, M931, grey green, M926, M927
gondolas: Black
posts: dark brown, M898

If you are using a different make of embroidery cotton, match up the colours on the picture.

15a   the centre palace

Method and order of working

1 Bind the canvas with masking tape.

2 Lay the canvas over the drawing of 'Venice' and trace the design on to the canvas, using an HB pencil or pale-coloured, waterproof fibre-tipped pen. Work the *centre palace* first. See diagram 15a.

3 Start with the roof. This comprises two rows of single trammed Gobelin stitch in M407, with one line of back stitch over 2 threads between the rows in M407, and another below the roof, continuing to form the upturned corners at each side, in M356.

4 The brickwork edges to the palace, the window frames and the divisions across the front of the palace, are tent stitch in M407. The sections where the brickwork projects into the Ecru centre portion are two straight stitches over one thread.

5 The windows are tent stitch in M317.

6 The top balconies are each two cross stitches over 3 threads in Ecru, with another cross over the top in 2 strands of M407. A total of six French knots in Ecru are placed in the arms of the crosses.

7 The lower balcony is made up of four cross stitches over 3 threads each (Ecru). Extra threads may be put in the needle to thicken these up, if desired.

8 The remainder of the front is worked in single brick stitch in Ecru.

9 The landing stages at the base of all the palaces are worked in single cross stitch in M642.

Palace on right See diagram 15b.

10 The gable of the roof is outlined in back stitch, and filled in with vertical satin stitch, in M356.

11 Underneath the roof windows is a line of back stitches over 2 threads in M407.

12 For the roof window frames in M642, follow the diagram.

13 The remainder of the roof is in tent stitch in M407.

14 The window frames are tent stitch in M762. The lower windows have a horizontal stitch over 2 threads to divide them in half.

15 The window panes are tent stitch in M317.

16 The balcony is three cross stitches, each over 4 threads, with 2 tramming threads underneath (both through the same middle holes) in M642.

17 The division across the middle of the palace is a line of tent stitches in M407.

18 The rest of the palace is worked in satin stitch over 2 diagonals (wherever possible) running from top left to bottom right.

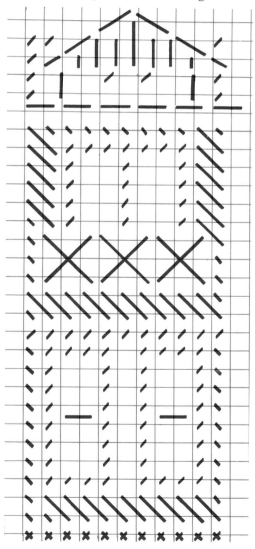

15b   the palace on the right

59

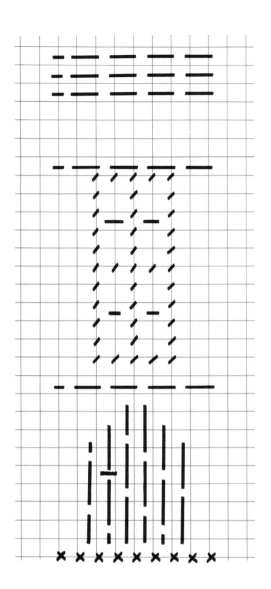

15c the palace on the left

Palace on left See diagram 15c.

19 The roof is three rows of back stitch over 2 threads in M356.

20 The divisions across the palace are back-stitch lines over 2 threads in M356.

21 The window frames are tent stitch in M356.

22 The window panes are each one Gobelin stitch in M317.

23 The door is twill stitch over 3 threads in M642; the door handle is one horizontal stitch in M356.

24 The rest of the palace is worked in single brick stitch placed sideways (M762).

25 The *sky* is Milanese stitch in M927.

26 The *Grand Canal* is worked randomly in long and short satin stitch, using the various shades of blue. (See instruction 10 of 'Lake scene' [page 27] for helpful hints.)

27 The *gondolas* are worked on top of the canal stitching. Follow diagram 15d. Extra strands of cotton may be added if coverage is not good.

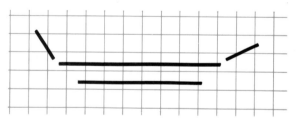

15d gondola

28 The *posts in the canal* are put on the surface last, each one being either a single straight stitch or two back stitches. Vary the length and make one or two of them lean slightly. Worked in M898.

29 *Finishing* follow the instructions in Chapter 3. When dry, have the miniature professionally mounted and framed unless you are very skilled yourself.

MARY QUEEN OF SCOTS' ELEPHANT

This cheerful elephant design was adapted from a larger embroidery, worked by Mary Queen of Scots in 1570 when she was held in captivity at Hardwick Hall in Derbyshire.

Materials

18s mono interlock canvas 5½ x 5 inches (14 x 12.5 cm)
Madeira 6-strand embroidery cottons, one pack of each colour, numbers as follows:

> *elephant*: fawn, M642, rose, M315, M316, Ecru, Black
> *background*: blue, M827, M334
> *foreground*: Ecru, blue, M824
> *cord edging*: blue, M824
> *corners*: green, M3013, rose, M315, M316, green, M367, yellow, M445, Ecru

If you are using a different make of embroidery cotton, match up the colours on the picture.

Method and order of working

1 Bind the canvas with masking tape.

2 Lay the canvas over the drawing of 'Mary Queen of Scots' elephant' and trace the design on to the canvas, using an HB pencil or pale-coloured, waterproof fibre-tipped pen.

3 Work the *elephant* first. Apart from the far legs and the ear, the body is worked in a mixture of three strands each of M642 and M316.
The far legs are worked in a mixture of three strands of M642, two of M315 and one of M316.
Work the ear first, in diagonal satin stitches across three diagonals in a wave pattern, as on diagram 16b, using compensation stitches where necessary. Graduate from M316 at the head end, through a mixture of three strands each of M315 and M316, to M315 alone at the back end.

62

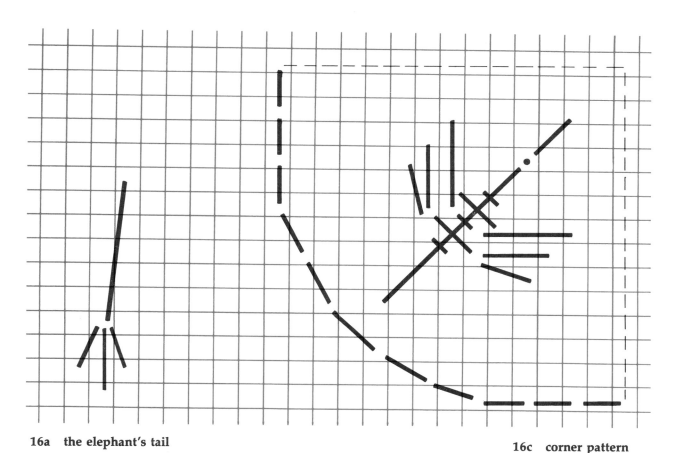

16a the elephant's tail

16c corner pattern

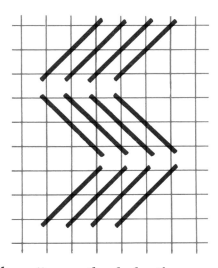

16b pattern on the elephant's ear

Hindquarters: cashmere stitch
Centre part: upright cross stitch
Front near leg and head: diagonal mosaic
stitch, sloping from top left to bottom right.
Far legs: basketweave tent stitch.
Tusk: a few overlapping straight stitches to fill
in the shape (Ecru).
Eye: one double French knot on top of the
diagonal mosaic stitch (Black).
Tail: one long stitch over 6 horizontal threads
and one vertical thread, with short stitches
forming the small tuft at the end (M315). See
diagram 16a.

4 *Top corners* work the back stitch edging first
(M315), then the bird (M315), and lastly the
single trammed Gobelin background in
alternate rows of Ecru and M3013. See
diagram 16c (right-hand corner). Reverse for
the left-hand corner.

63

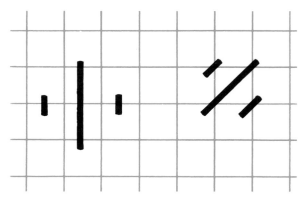

16d the leaves

5 *Lower corners* work the back-stitch edging as for the top corners, allowing for the elephant's leg on the left-hand side.
The flowers are French knots in M445, M315 and M316. The stems are single straight stitches in M367, and the leaves are upright or diagonal groups of three stitches over 1, 3, 1 threads or 1, 2, 1 diagonals. See diagram 16d. The single trammed Gobelin background is worked as above, step 4.

6 *Background* mosaic stitch, blending down from M827 alone at the top, through a mixture of three strands each of M827 and M334, to M334 on its own at the bottom.

7 *Foreground* the dark blue pattern is worked randomly in tent stitch (M824) to simulate crazy tiling, and the centre portions are filled in with basketweave tent stitch (Ecru).

8 *Cord edging* work one row of long-legged cross variation all round the edge (M824). Outside this, work one row of tent stitch (M824) to help the framer to fit the mount close up to the long-legged cross cord.

9 *Finishing* follow the instructions in Chapter 3. When dry, have the miniature professionally mounted and framed unless you are very skilled yourself.

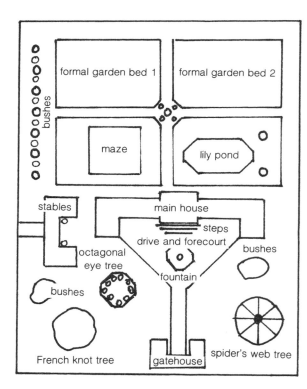

This stylized plan of a manor house surrounded by its park and formal gardens, provides an opportunity to work several stitches not used elsewhere in the projects. To save a lot of counting of threads, the main features are purposely placed off-centre, so positioning of the various outlines is not critical.

Materials

18s mono interlock canvas 5¾ x 5 inches (14.5 x 12.5 cm)
Madeira 6-strand embroidery cottons, one pack of each colour, numbers as follows:

> Greens: M500, M501, M502, M503, M3072
> Pinks: M315, M316, M778
> Yellow: M445

If you are using a different make of embroidery cotton, match up the colours on the picture.

Method and order of working

1 Bind the canvas with masking tape.

2 Lay the canvas over the drawing of 'Manor house and formal gardens' and trace the design on to the canvas, using an HB pencil or pale-coloured, waterproof fibre-tipped pen.

3 Work the **main house** first. The centre square is a Norwich stitch over 7 threads (M315). Two of the 7 threads project in front of the main block, and one behind. To achieve the best effect with this stitch, twist the thread so that it is more like a cord.

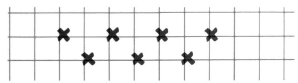

17a   the pond surround

4 ***Wings of the house*** rice stitches, with the basic crosses in M315. The corners of alternate stitches are crossed with M316 and M778.

5 ***Stable block*** a rice stitch (M778 crossed with M315) forms each wing. For the back, work seven cross stitches over two diagonals (M778). Alternate cross stitches have an upright cross in M315 on top.

6 ***Paths between the formal garden beds*** cross stitch over two diagonals (M3072). Start each path from the central area to make sure they all meet properly. Work one double French knot, surrounded by four single French knots (M445), where the paths meet.

7 ***Hedges round formal garden beds*** single French knots (M501) made across one thread of the canvas on the straight sides, but into each hole on the short diagonal edges. Be careful not to pull the knot through the holes here.

8 ***Maze*** satin square over 9 threads (M500). See Stitch directory.

9 ***To right and left of the maze*** vertical lines of single trammed Gobelin stitch, with alternate stitches in M503 and M316. Make single French knots (M316) along the other two sides of the maze.

10 ***Lily pond*** satin stitch (M3072) over 2, 4, 6, 6, 6, 6, 6, 6, 6, 6, 4, 2, horizontal threads.

11 ***Round the lily pond*** edge the pond with single cross stitches (M500). Two double French knots (M500) form bushes at the outer end. The rest of the area is filled with single cross stitches (M316) over every other intersection. See diagram 17a.

12 ***Formal garden bed 1*** web stitch. The diagonal lines are laid down in M502, and the cross bars are worked in M778.

13 ***Formal garden bed 2*** diamond straight stitch. The main motifs are in M316, and the surrounding single stitches are in M502. Three rows of whole motifs with a half row at the top and bottom will fit the space exactly. Start by working a row of whole motifs, and go back to fill in the halves later.

14 ***Bushes along the left-hand side of the formal garden beds*** seven double French knots in M316 are worked over one thread, and have 3 threads in between each knot. To position correctly, start with the middle knot placed opposite the end of the path. Place single French knots in M445 between the larger knots.

15 ***Gatehouse*** three cross stitches over three diagonals (M315), with back stitches (M778) all round. See diagram 17b.

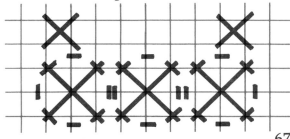

17b the gatehouse   67

A cross stitch (M315) over 2 diagonals is placed at each end on the house side.

16 **Steps in front of the main house** three satin stitches (M316) over 9, 7 and 5 vertical threads form the steps in front of the Norwich stitch.

17 **Fountain in front of the steps** a triple French knot (three times round the needle) in M315, surrounded by back stitches, as shown on the diagram below.

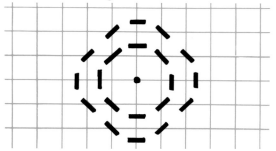

17c   the fountain

18 Outline the **drive and forecourt area** in front of the main house and the **short drive to the stable block** in M501, by working a running stitch in and out over one thread on the straight sections, and over one intersection on the diagonal sections. Make a double French knot between each running stitch (M501). Work a double French knot in M445 at the two front corners of the main house, and two more where the wings of the stable block meet the back.

19 **Forecourt and drives** work random French knots in three strands only of M3072, interspersed with a few similar knots in M445.

20 **Tree on right of gatehouse** a spider's web stitch over 5 threads on the verticals and horizontals, and over 4 intersections on the diagonals (M500). Make a French knot in the centre (M316), and surround the whole stitch with French knots in M445.

21 **Tree to left of gatehouse** closely packed French knots in M500, with about seven knots each of M315 and M445.

22 **Octagonal eye stitch tree** (M501), with a central French knot (M445), and French knots in each segment in M316.

23 **French knot bushes** the two groups of bushes are French knots in M316, M502 and M445.

24 **Background to the parkland** single brick stitch (M503). Start working at the top of the picture, so that several rows are worked before dividing round the formal garden beds. This ensures that the stitches will match up again when they meet by the main house.

25 A **fence** between back and front areas of the parkland is shown by running a thread of M500 under alternate single brick stitches, level with the back of the main house.

26 Work round the entire picture in long-legged cross stitch variation, using M445. Outside this, work one row of tent stitch to help the framer fit the mount close up to the long-legged cross stitching.

27 **Finishing** follow the instructions in Chapter 3. When dry, have the miniature professionally mounted and framed unless you are very skilled yourself.

10 MICRO MINIATURES: LONELY SAIL AND SPRINGTIME

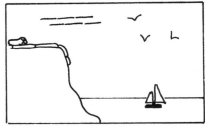

These postage stamp size miniatures are easy to work and can be finished in an evening. They are also easy to design, and something similar might be a good starting point for branching out on your own. The right choice of colour and stitch is vital in such a tiny piece of work. It is best to avoid any of the very large stitches.

4 **Grass** four or five back-stitches along the top of the cliff, and about ¼ inch (.6 cm) over the edge (M367). If you want to put the sheep on the clifftop, work it in two single cross stitches (M640), with two small, straight stitches (M898) for the head, as in Chapter 6.

5 **Boat** work the sails as two small triangles (White), and the hull as a single straight stitch (M898). See diagram 18a.

6 **Sky** chevron stitch over 3 threads in each direction (M927).

7 **Clouds** two rows of three small back-stitches in White, worked on top of the sky.

8 **Birds** V-shapes (on top of chevron stitches) made up of two small straight stitches, using three strands only of M898.

9 **Sea** random long and short stitches (M930 and M931). See note on working long and short satin stitches in 'Lake scene' (page 27).

10 **Finishing** follow the instructions in Chapter 3. When dry, have the miniature professionally mounted and framed unless you are very skilled yourself.

Lonely sail
Materials

18s mono interlock canvas 4 x 3 inches (10 x 7.5 cm)
Madeira 6-strand embroidery cottons, one pack of each colour, numbers as follows:

sky: grey-blue, M927
cloud and sails: White
hull of boat, birds and head of sheep: dark brown, M898
sea: blues, M930 and M931
cliff and sheep: grey-brown, M640
grass: green, M367

If using a different make of embroidery cotton, match up the colours on the picture.

Method and order of working

1 Bind the canvas with masking tape.

2 Lay the canvas over the drawing of 'Lonely sail', being careful to line up the top of the cliff and the skyline along threads of the canvas, and trace the design on to the canvas, using an HB pencil or pale-coloured, waterproof fibre-tipped pen.

3 Work the *cliff* first in crossed Gobelin stitch (M640). At the bottom you will not have room for the complete Gobelin stitch, but you will have enough to include the crosses.

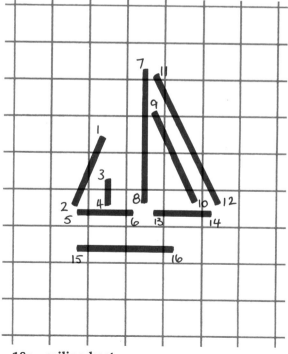

18a   sailing boat

Springtime

Materials

18s mono interlock canvas 4 x 3 inches (10 x 7.5 cm)

Madeira 6-strand embroidery cottons, one pack of each colour, numbers as follows:

clouds: White
sky: grey-blue, M932
hillside: green, M368
tree: green, M369 and pink, M963; trunk: brown, M898
sheep: White and brown, M898
grass hummocks: green, M369
flowers: White and yellow, M445

If using a different make of embroidery cotton, match up the colours in the picture.

Method and order of working

1 Bind the canvas with masking tape.

2 Lay the canvas over the drawing of 'Springtime', being careful to line up the base of the cloud with a strand of the canvas, and trace the design on to the canvas, using an HB pencil or pale-coloured, waterproof fibre-tipped pen.

3 Work the *tree* first, in French knots (M369) with flowers (M963). Trunk: single cross stitch (M898).

4 *Grassy hummocks* vertical satin stitches of varying length (M369).

5 *Hillside* diagonal ground stitch (M368), sloping from top right to bottom left, putting in the sheep as you come to them. They are two French knots (White), and the heads are two small straight stitches (M898), as for the sheep in Chapter 6 (page 24).

6 *Clouds* vertical satin stitches in White. The left-hand portion may be sewn in two tiers to give added effect. See Chapter 6 (page 24).

7 *Sky* double twill stitch (M932) from top left to bottom right. The rows alternate between being sewn over 3 threads and over 2 threads.

8 *Flowers* French knots in yellow (M445) and White. Follow the picture.

9 *Finishing* follow the instructions in Chapter 3. When dry, have the miniature professionally mounted and framed unless you are very skilled yourself.

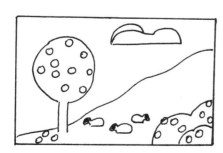

19 SHADES OF PINK

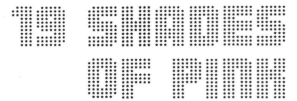

A student of the author designed and made a most effective cushion, covered entirely in pink needlepoint flowerheads. This design has something of the same 'feel' and, besides being very pretty, gives an opportunity to try out many different flower and leaf shapes in needlepoint.

Materials

18s mono interlock canvas 4½ inches square (11.5 x 11.5 cm)
Madeira 6-strand embroidery cottons, one pack of each colour, numbers as follows:

> *flowers*: rose, M223, magenta, M601, pink, M3354, M962, lilac, M3042, dark and light rose, M3350, M3687, pink, M3689.
> *leaves*: greens, M367, M368
> *background*: green, M367

If you are using a different make of embroidery cotton, match up the colours on the picture.

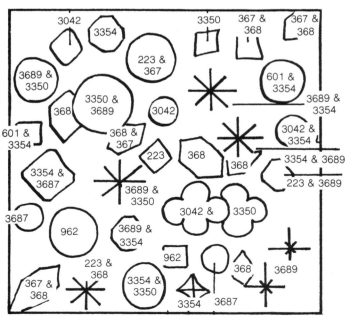

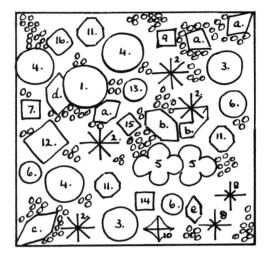

Method

1 Bind the canvas with masking tape.

2 There is no need to mark the position of each flower on the canvas, as they are randomly placed. If you want your finished product to look like the picture, then work the flowers and leaves in the same colour threads and in approximately the same places — a few threads in any direction will not make a great deal of difference. See diagram above for positions, and diagrams overleaf for stitches not in the stitch directory. Work the flowers in any order, placing French knots in the centres where appropriate. When the leaves have been worked in one colour, a few of the stitches may be worked over again in a different shade of green (three strands only) to give added interest.

3 When all the flowers and leaves have been placed, add random groups of French knots, then work the background in tent stitch with M367.

4 *Finishing* follow the instructions in Chapter 3. When dry, have the miniature professionally mounted and framed unless you are very skilled yourself. This design would look equally good if used as the top of a pincushion. In this case, it would probably be best to stretch the work by dampening the back before pulling into shape, rather than to use the paste.

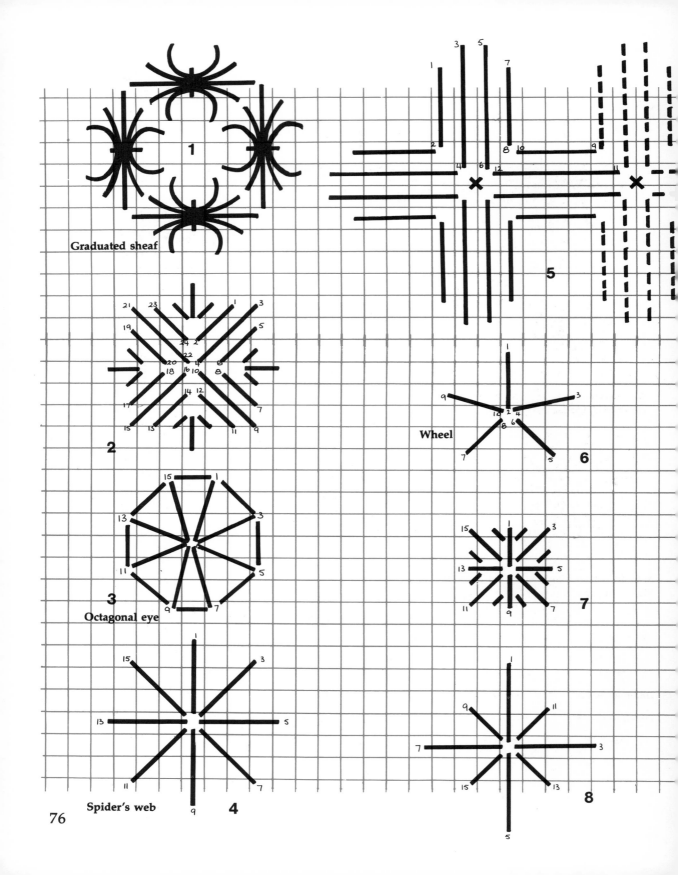

1

Graduated sheaf

2

3 Octagonal eye

Spider's web **4**

5

Wheel **6**

7

8

can be
worked
facing
four ways

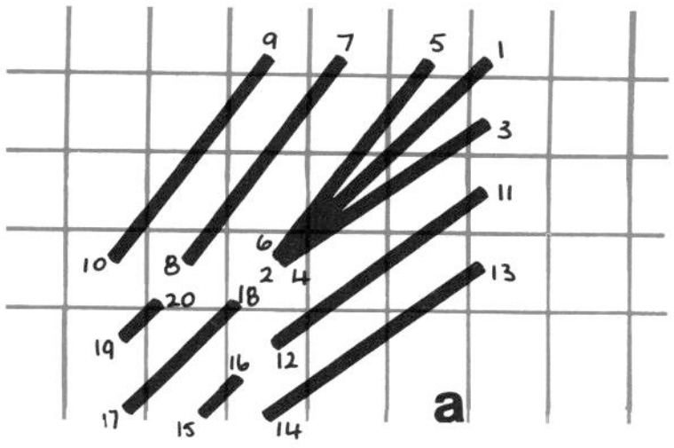

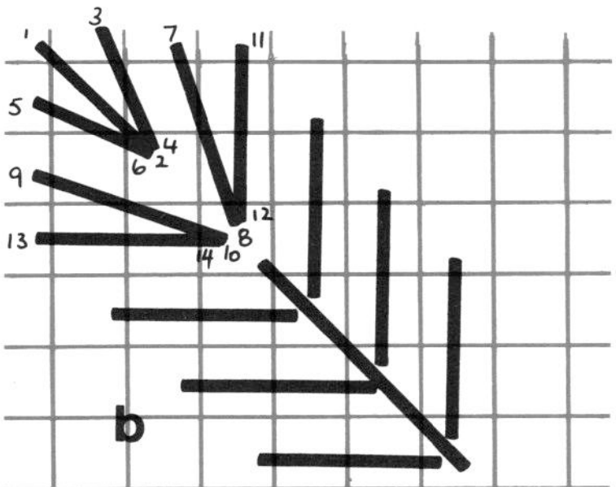

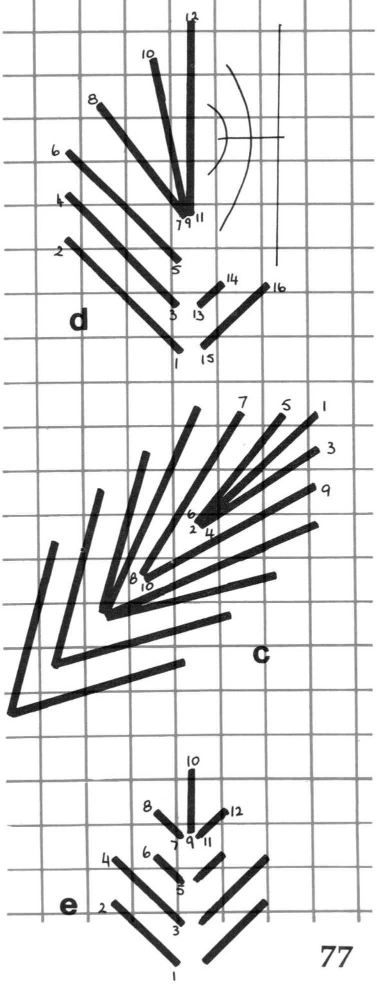

Graduated sheaf

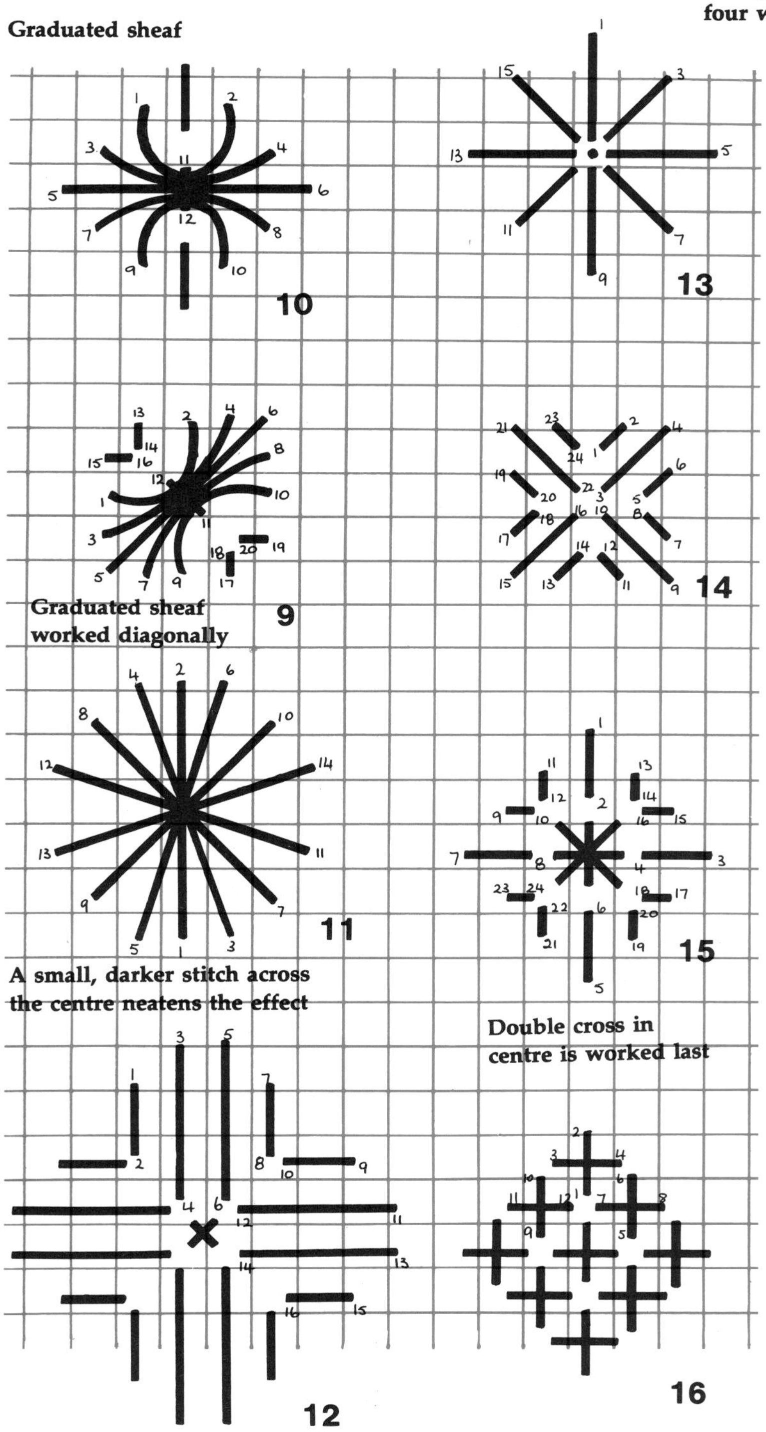

10

9

**Graduated sheaf
worked diagonally**

11

A small, darker stitch across
the centre neatens the effect

12

13

14

15

Double cross in
centre is worked last

16

a

b

d

c

e

77

20 HINTS ON MOUNTING & FRAMING

Some people will probably want to mount and frame their own pieces of needlepoint, and will already have the skills with which to do this. If you have never done anything in this line, it is probably better to take the work to a professional framer, rather than run the risk of doing a poor job and perhaps ruining the whole effect. As the pieces are so small, professional framing need not be too costly.

Mounts

The first pictures which were done as models for this book were placed in mounts which picked out or toned with one of the paler colours in the picture. This seemed to look alright, but did little to enhance the scenes. Later on, when one or two of the models were repeated, they were mounted in dark mounts, and this had the effect of distancing the scenes and making them much more dramatic and interesting.

When a mount is cut by a professional it has a bevelled edge, and this is usually a creamy white, as the outer colour of the mount does not go through the whole board. For some of the miniatures it was decided that this pale border would be distracting, so it was painted over with a watercolour paint which matched the mount as far as possible. This was done, for example, with 'Lake scene', see facing page, top left.

Some of the designs which have stitches incorporated into them such as French knots, spiders' webs, and wheels, end up being quite three-dimensional, and it is important that in the process of framing the glass does not press down on these raised stitches. The thickness of the mount may be enough to raise the glass sufficiently, but if there is any doubt it is a good idea to have a double mount, the second one being a little less than ¼ inch (.6 cm) outside the first. These mounts do not need to be the same colour, and you will be surprised how different pictures look when the mounts are changed. 'Winter evening' (page 53) and 'Lonely sail' (page 72) have double mounts of different colours, while 'Springtime' (page 72) has a double mount of the same colour. Even if the subject is not three-dimensional, a double mount will often give it added importance, particularly with the smaller designs.

Another decision which has to be taken is how wide to make the mounts. The framer will usually have a wealth of experience and it is often best to leave the decisions to him; however, you may have definite ideas of your own about whether you want the finished miniature to be in a fairly small frame, or whether you want it isolated in the middle of a large expanse of mount. A compromise of about 1¼ inches (3 cms) at the sides and top of a rectangular miniature, with a little more at the bottom, may well be the answer. The ovals in the book have about 1 inch (2.5 cm) of mount showing at the narrowest point of the sides, and 1¼ inches (3 cms) at the bottom.

Frames

Frames must be chosen to suit the subject but also, if possible, the place where the picture will hang. Most of the subjects in this book have been placed in a fairly narrow and simple gilt moulding, which would look at home in most environments, except, perhaps, in very modern surroundings.

The 'Country house' (page 49) was framed in a brown wood which matched the mount, with only a narrow gilt band, so that there should be no distraction from the pale subject matter.

Only one modern frame was chosen, that for 'Shades of pink' (page 75). This subject would have looked quite wrong in a gilt frame, and, having selected a pink mount as showing off the subject to best advantage, the only possible choice for the frame seemed to be green, which was the other dominant colour.

Take plenty of time choosing your mounts and mouldings, as they will have a great effect on the finished appearance of your piece of needlepoint.

21 STITCH DIRECTORY

There are hundreds of different needlepoint stitches, including many variations, but only the ones used in the projects and the Special Effects chapter are·listed here. Even so, this comprises nearly fifty stitches and gives great scope for combination and variety.

Note that all diagonal stitches may be worked down the opposite diagonal from that illustrated.

Back	Gobelin, Knotted	Parisian
Brick	Gobelin, Single	Parisian, Small
Double Brick	trammed	Rhodes
Single Brick	Graduated Sheaf	Rice
Byzantine	Hungarian 1	Satin
Cashmere	Hungarian 2	Satin Square
Chevron	Jacquard	Spider's Web
Cross	Lattice	Tent, Diagonal or
Cross, Double	Leaf	Basketweave
Cross, Single	Long-legged	Tent, Continental
Cross, Upright	Cross	Tramming thread
Diagonal	Long-legged	Twill
Ground	Cross variation	Double Twill
Diamond	Milanese	Weaving
Straight	Mosaic	Web
Florentine	Mosaic, Diagonal	Wheel
French Knot	Norwich	
Gobelin	Oblique Slav	
Gobelin,	Octagonal Eye	
Crossed	Oriental	

Back This is mainly used for outlining areas where other stitches would either be too bulky, or could not be worked in the required direction. Back stitch is usually worked over 2 threads, but can be worked over more or fewer, if required.

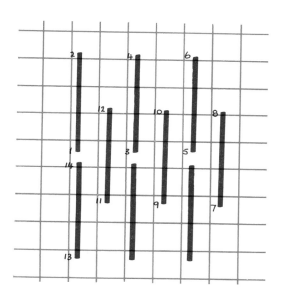

brick

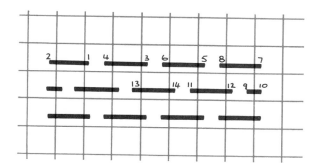

back

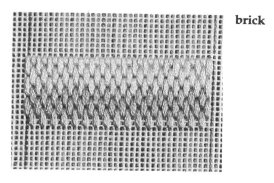

Brick This is usually worked over 4 threads and may be used vertically or horizontally. As the second row comes half-way up the first, different colours or shades can be worked in very effectively. The small gaps left at the top should be filled in with half-size compensation stitches.

Brick — double Two upright stitches are worked alongside each other to give a very different effect from brick stitch. Do not forget to leave a gap two holes wide between uprights for the second row stitches.

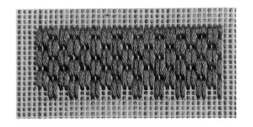

Brick — single This is worked over 2 horizontal threads instead of 4. It makes a neat background stitch, as well as being very useful for roofs, walls, etc.

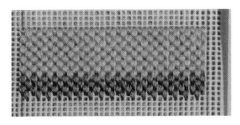

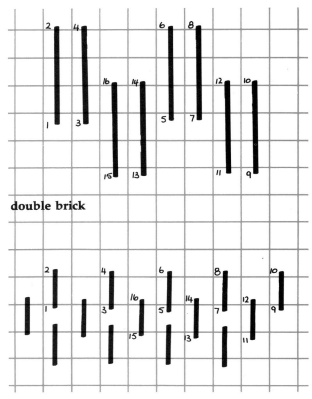

double brick

single brick

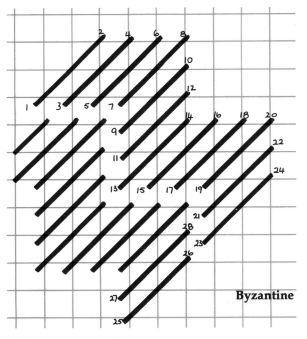

Byzantine

Byzantine This stitch consists of parallel diagonal satin stitches worked in steps of the same width. Byzantine stitch can be worked randomly to achieve special effects, such as crazy paving.

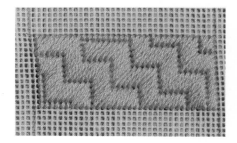

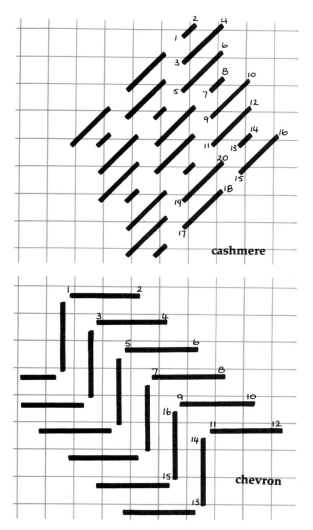

cashmere

Cashmere This is a useful diagonal stitch which runs at a steeper angle than the straight diagonal line. It can thus be used as a contrast with most other stitches. The stitch consists of one short stitch over one intersection, with two longer stitches beneath over two intersections. The next short stitch is then placed to the right of the lower long stitch. Cashmere is not an easy stitch to work without careful attention, but the finished result is worth some effort.

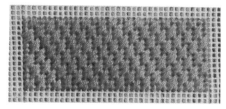

Chevron The two parts of this stitch are worked at right angles to each other, along the horizontal and vertical threads, giving the finished appearance of a diagonal stitch. It can be worked over 3 or 4 threads of the canvas. This stitch is effective as a sky, especially as the light catching the silks gives a two-tone look.

chevron

Cross This is worked over two intersections of the canvas. It is usual to have all the top diagonals running in the same direction.

cross

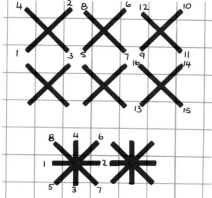

double cross

Cross — double An upright cross is made over 2 threads, and then an ordinary diagonal cross is stitched over the top. This makes a three-dimensional stitch.

83

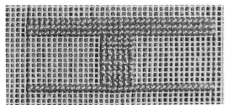

single cross

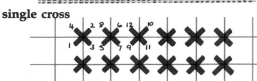

Cross — single This stitch is worked over a single intersection of the canvas, and has almost the appearance of tent stitch, but is very firm and knobbly. It is usual to have all the top diagonals running in the same direction.

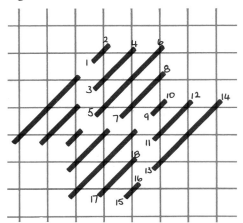

diagonal ground

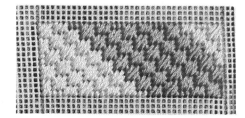

Diagonal ground Stitches are made across 1, 2, 3, 2, intersections of the canvas, and then repeated. The long stitch of the second row fits against the short stitch of the first. Diagonal ground makes a smooth surface which catches the light well.

84

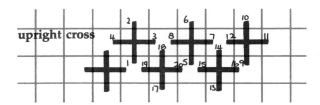

upright cross

Cross — upright This is worked across 2 threads in each direction. The second row fits neatly between the upright stitches of the row above. Upright cross stitch can be formed into attractive geometrical shapes to represent bushes and trees.

Diamond straight This can be worked in either one or two colours. The diamond consists of straight stitches over 1, 3, 5, 3, 1 threads. On the second row, the diamonds are placed between the ones above. Small, straight stitches over one thread are placed all round the diamonds, possibly in another colour.

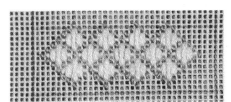

diamond straight

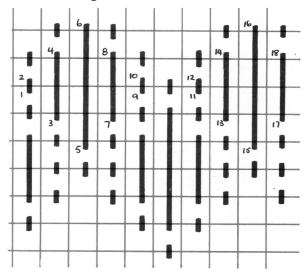

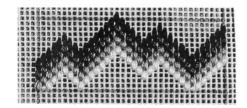

Florentine Straight stitches are worked adjacent to each other, usually in a regular pattern of ups and downs. In these miniatures, however, Florentine is more often worked in random patterns to simulate flames, or groups of rocks in a foreground. If the finished work will be behind glass, stitches may be quite long, but tension must be taut and even.

French knot These knots can be used to achieve many different effects, either singly or massed together. They must be made correctly to avoid the unprofessional look of the knot dangling on a loose thread. Proceed as follows:

1 Bring the needle up where you require the knot.
2 Hold the yarn as it comes out of the canvas about ¾ inch (2 cm) away from the canvas with your left hand. Keep the yarn fairly taut.
3 For a small knot, twist the needle round the yarn once; for a large knot, twice.
4 Still holding the yarn taut, move the needle with the yarn twisted round it down towards the canvas, and insert the needle in to an adjacent hole if it is a small knot, or the same hole if a large knot. (The large knot will not slip through the hole.)
5 Keep hold of the yarn with the left hand as you pull the needle and yarn through the knot. Make sure the knot is resting on the canvas as the needle is pulled through.

Florentine

French knot

hold thread — needle under yarn
— needle over yarn
stage 1
stage 2 — knot resting on canvas
hold thread

Gobelin The basic Gobelin stitch is worked over one vertical thread and 2 horizontal threads. It is rather like a large tent-stitch. A larger stitch may be worked over 4 horizontal threads.

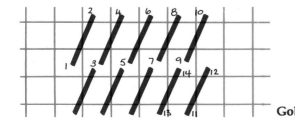

Gobelin

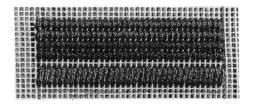

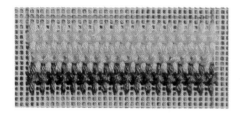

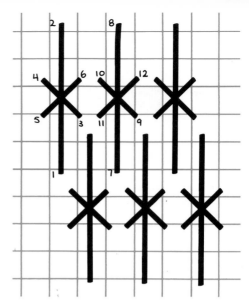

crossed
Gobelin

Gobelin — crossed This Gobelin stitch is combined with a cross stitch, which adds a more three-dimensional effect. A long upright stitch is worked over 6 threads of canvas, and then a cross stitch is placed over the centre 2 threads in each direction. On the second row, the long stitch is worked into the hole where the cross stitches meet.

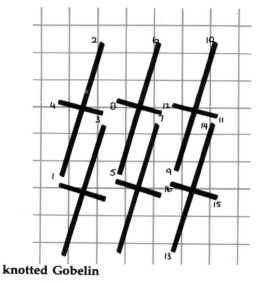

knotted Gobelin

Gobelin — knotted This is a well textured, sloping stitch. It is worked over 5 horizontal and 2 vertical threads, and is tied down across the centre by a slanting stitch over 2 vertical threads, and one horizontal thread of the canvas. Two threads of canvas are left between each stitch to leave room for the top of the stitches in the row below.

Gobelin — single trammed This neat three-dimensional stitch is very useful in landscapes to represent ploughed fields, rough pasture, roofs with rounded tiles, and so on. It may be worked either horizontally or vertically. Proceed as follows:
1 Lay down a tramming thread (i.e. a single long thread along the front of the work), between the 2 threads of canvas you intend to use for the stitch. Tramming threads may be almost any length within reason, but if working without a frame, great care must be taken to ensure that the yarn lies smoothly on the canvas. It must not pull the canvas or lie slackly.
2 Stitch vertically over the tramming thread into each hole, thus working over 2 horizontal canvas threads.
3 Lay down the next tramming thread and repeat the stitch. Always work the same way along the row or else the vertical stitches will lie slightly differently.

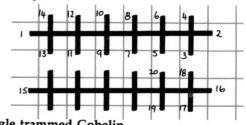

single trammed Gobelin

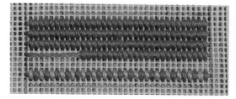

graduated sheaf

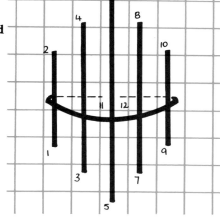

Graduated sheaf This is a useful stitch for many different special effects, and can be used either vertically or horizontally. Proceed as follows:

1 Work upright stitches over 4, 6, 8, 6, 4 horizontal canvas threads.

2 Carefully pull the long middle stitch to the left with your nail, and bring the needle and thread right out through the exposed centre hole.

3 Slide the needle and thread under the three left-hand stitches and pull taut.

4 Insert the needle under the two right-hand stitches and push down into the centre hole under the long stitch, thus encircling the 'sheaf'.

5 Pull tightly to 'bind' the sheaf.

A smaller sheaf may be worked over 2, 4, 6, 4, 2 canvas threads.

Hungarian 2 This has a very neat appearance, suitable for lawns and gravel areas, etc. It can also be used for diamond-paned leaded windows, if a back stitch is placed between the motifs. Proceed as follows:

1 Work vertical stitches over 2, 4, 2 horizontal canvas threads.

2 Leave 2 bare threads (one hole) before repeating the group of three stitches.

3 On the return row the long stitch is worked into the hole left empty.

N.B. Unlike **Hungarian 1** all the long stitches come under each other and similarly all the short stitches.

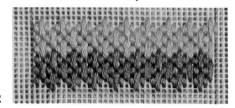

Hungarian 2

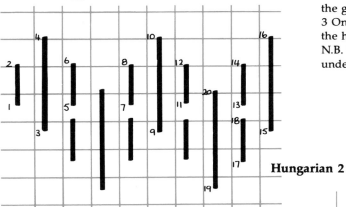

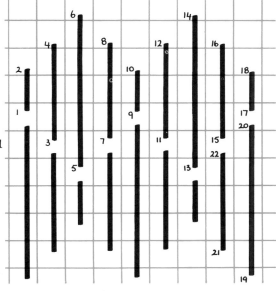

Hungarian 1

Hungarian 1 Work vertical stitches over 2, 4, 6, 4, horizontal canvas threads, and repeat. The short stitch of the next row fits under the long stitch of the row above.

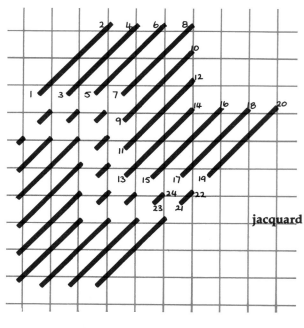

jacquard

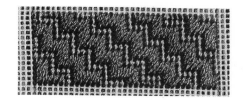

Jacquard This is especially interesting worked in two colours. The first row is satin stitch worked diagonally in steps of the same width over, say, three diagonals. The next row follows the steps exactly, but is done in tent stitch, possibly in a different colour.

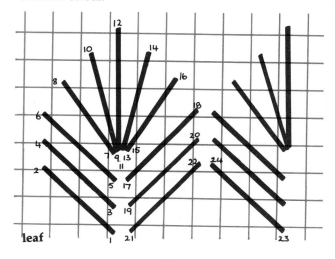

leaf

lattice

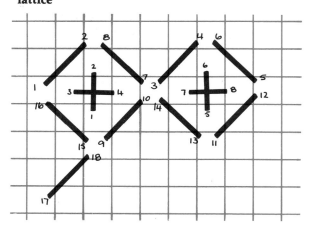

Lattice This stitch makes very neat diamond shapes, which in miniatures can be used for diamond-paned leaded windows. The diamond shape is filled in with three diagonal satin stitches, or an upright cross stitch.

Leaf This is one of the more three-dimensional stitches and may be used singly, or several can be put together in various ways for different effects. French knots or stems may be added for further variety.

Follow the sequence of numbers on the diagram carefully, and note that the middle hole where the leaf fans out is used five times. When working the second half of the leaf, the holes tend to be masked by the thread, and care must be taken to find the correct hole.

88

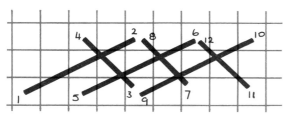

long-legged cross

Long-legged cross This is a very useful stitch for edgings, as it has a plaited appearance and is a firm stitch for sewing into. If two or three rows are worked, the canvas can be made to bend down the side of, say, a kneeler or pincushion between the rows (if two rows), or with one row on the edge (if three rows). To make a flat end at the beginning of the row, an extra cross must be made first at this point.

Long-legged cross variation This is a slightly smaller variation of long-legged cross, which makes a cord-like edging when worked in stranded cottons.

long-legged cross variation

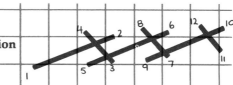

Milanese This is a very effective sky stitch, but the full wavy pattern can only be seen if a fairly large area is worked. Note that the long stitch of one row abuts against the short stitches of the ones on either side (unlike Oriental stitch).

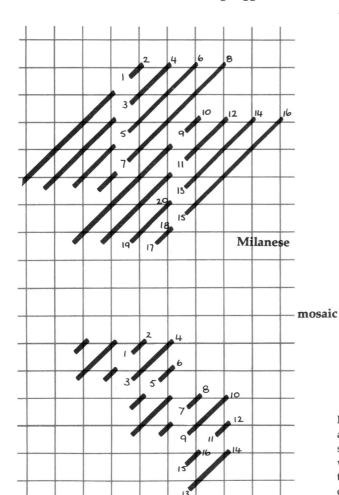

Milanese

mosaic

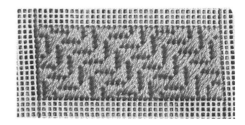

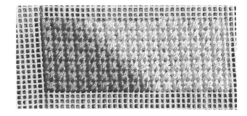

Mosaic This stitch is most easily worked diagonally, and the finished effect is not unlike neat cross stitches. The stitches are formed in groups of three, with a gap in between into which the long stitch of the next row is placed. Note that all the long diagonal stitches are in line with each other.

Mosaic — diagonal This is probably the simplest of the diagonal stitches, with the long stitch over 2 diagonals fitting neatly up against the short stitch of the previous row.

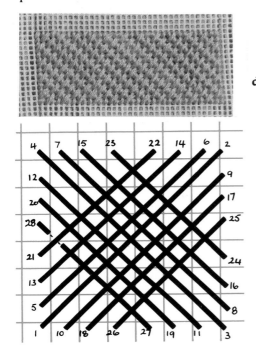

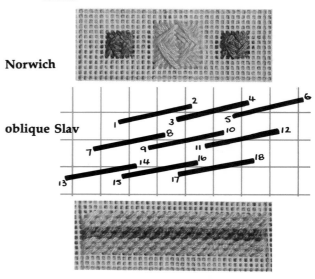

diagonal mosaic

Norwich This stitch must be worked over an uneven number of canvas threads, and should be quite large to show to advantage. Follow the numbers carefully until you understand the make-up of this stitch. The very last hole is entered by passing the needle under instead of over the thread next to it. Norwich stitch looks best worked in a tightly spun yarn, such as perle or twisted stranded cotton.

Norwich

oblique Slav

Oblique Slav This stitch gives a gently sloping appearance, which is very useful where differing hillside gradients are needed. It is easiest to work every row from the left-hand end, each row starting one thread further to the left than the previous one. Thus the right-hand ends of the second row of stitches go into the same holes as the left-hand ends of the first row.

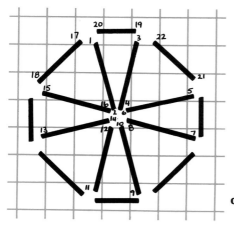

Octagonal eye Eight stitches are worked into the centre hole as shown on the diagram. Back stitches are then worked round the edge into the ends of the spokes. French knots may be placed in each triangle formed, and in the centre.

octagonal eye

Oriental This is a more complex form of Milanese stitch and has to be worked carefully, especially when compensation stitches are required. It is usually easier to put in the main stitch before attempting to put in the small compensation stitches. Proceed as follows:

1 Work a row of arrowheads down the diagonal over 1, 2, 3 and 4 intersections.
2 Place single stitches over 2 diagonals against all but the longest stitches of the previous row.
3 Work arrowheads as in row 1, but facing the opposite direction.
Note that the long stitches of the arrowheads abut against each other.

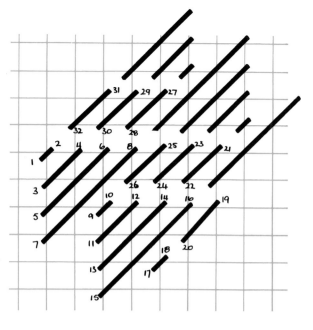

oriental

Parisian Straight stitches over 6 and 2 horizontal threads. These may be used sideways if required.

Parisian

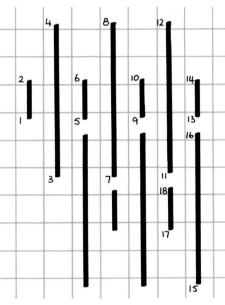

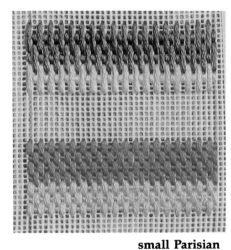

small Parisian

Parisian — small Work straight stitches over 3 and 1 horizontal threads.

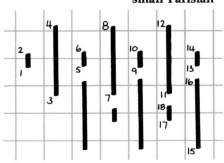

91

Rhodes This can be made almost any size within reason, but its character cannot be appreciated if it is too small. Starting with one diagonal, stitches are made across the centre of the square into every hole round the edge. A small stitch may be made across the middle of the completed stitch to hold the long threads down.

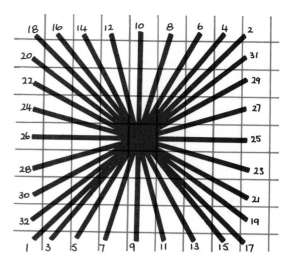

Rhodes

rice

Rice This is a square stitch and, as such, is not often used for landscape effects. A large single cross is made across 4 diagonals, and then each corner is crossed from one middle hole to the other round the square, usually in another colour.

Satin This name is given to a vast number of different patterns made with parallel straight stitches, either vertical, horizontal or diagonal. Satin stitches catch the light very well, especially worked in embroidery cottons. Tension must be kept even and the stitches worked in an 'over and over' fashion.

satin

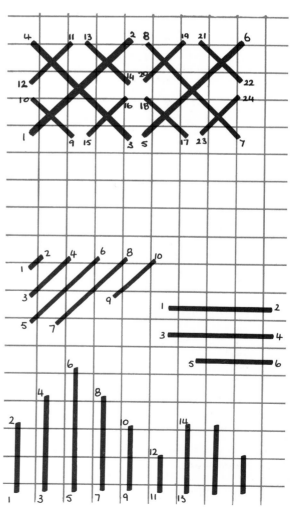

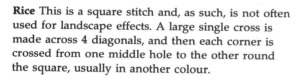

92

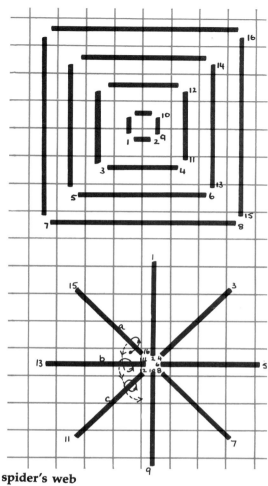

spider's web

Satin square A single satin square is formed by working 4 sets of satin stitch triangles at right angles to each other. The square may be of any size. To make a background of satin squares, the longest stitch of each side of the square is made the longest stitch of one side of an adjacent square.

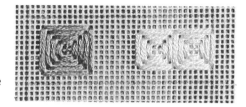

satin square

Spider's web This is the most textured stitch featured, and is worked almost entirely on the surface of the canvas. The spider's web may be made in different sizes, although anything covering a diameter of less than 6 threads will be difficult to work and not look very dramatic. Make sure you have a long enough thread to finish the whole stitch and proceed as follows:

1 Work the basic 8 stitches *into* the central hole, keeping a firm tension.
2 Bring the needle and thread out between threads a and b on the diagram.
3 Take the thread back over the top of a and then forward under a and b (coming out between b and c).
4 Take the thread back over the top of b and forward under b and c.
5 Continue in this way until the whole web is filled. Note that the needle does not go through to the back of the canvas after the initial star has been made until the web is finished.

When the radius is over 8 canvas threads, the diagonal thread, to be the same length, must only be taken over six canvas intersections.

Tent — diagonal or basketweave This stitch can be used to fill in even small areas in preference to continental tent stitch. It is slightly more difficult to master, but if you find it hard to see where to place the stitches, run along the diagonals in different coloured felt tips when you practise.

diagonal or basketweave tent

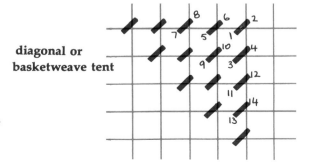

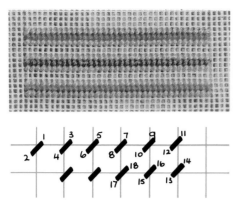

continental tent

Tent — Continental Tent stitch is the smallest diagonal needlepoint stitch, and can be used very effectively as a smooth background for the more three-dimensional stitches. Continental tent stitch should be used sparingly as it quickly pulls the canvas out of shape. It is useful for outlining.

Do not mix the two types of tent stitch in one area, as the finished appearance, though very similar, is not the same.

tramming thread

Tramming thread This is a thread laid down along the line the stitching is to take, the stitches being made over it. It is used either to strengthen the finished work or to give it added texture.

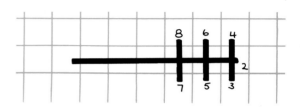

Twill This is an attractive stitch for skies, worked in one or two colours. It must be worked over 3 or more horizontal canvas threads with a drop of one or 2 threads, as, if worked over 2 threads with a single drop, it looks exactly like single brick stitch.

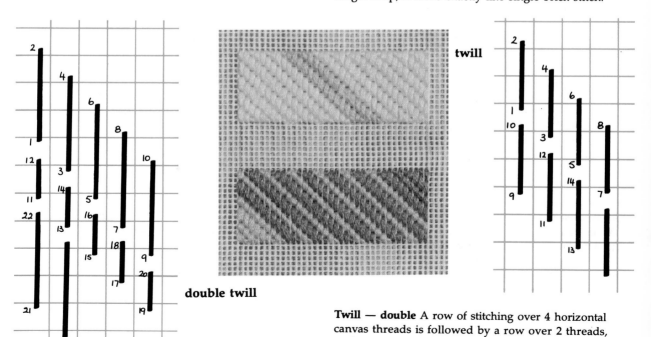

twill

double twill

Twill — double A row of stitching over 4 horizontal canvas threads is followed by a row over 2 threads, perhaps in a contrasting or toning colour.

94

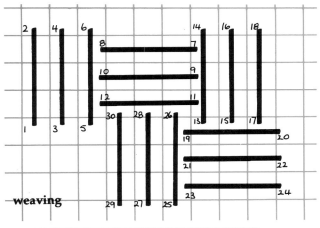

weaving

Weaving The stitch simulates a woven appearance and may be done in two colours to accentuate this. It is easier, though heavier on thread, to work towards the stitches already in position. Proceed as follows:

1 Three upright stitches are worked over 4 horizontal threads of canvas.

2 Three horizontal stitches are worked across 4 vertical canvas threads into the holes under the last of the upright stitches.

Be careful not to split the yarn of the stitches already in position.

3 On the second row, the upright stitches are worked into three holes under the lowest horizontal stitch, and the first of the horizontal stitches is worked across the end of the upright stitches.

Web Long threads are laid diagonally across alternate holes of the canvas. After each thread has been laid, it is tied down with a matching or contrasting thread coming up through every other hole along its length. On the next row the tying down threads are put between those of the previous row to give a woven appearance.

web

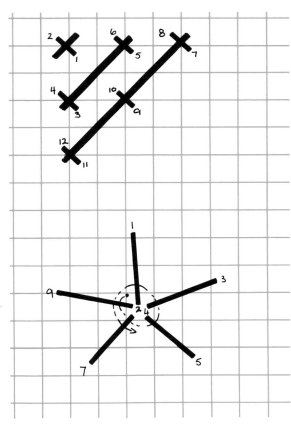

Wheel An initial star is laid down, similar to the Spider's Web stitch, but with only five spokes, all stitched into the centre. The thread is then brought up between any two of the arms and taken over and under alternate arms, without going through to the back of the work, until a raised knob is formed.

wheel

Bibliography

Baker, Muriel, et al *Needlepoint: Design Your Own*, New York 1977

Christensen, Jo Ippolito *The Needlepoint Book*, New York 1986

Good Housekeeping *Needlepoint*, London 1981

Gray, Jennifer *Canvas Work*, London 1985

Hanley, Hope *101 Needlepoint Stitches & how to use them*, New York 1986

Kurten, Nancy N. *Needlepoint: Stitch by Stitch*, New York 1977

Pearson, Anna *First Steps in Needlepoint*, London 1985

Rhodes, Mary *Needlepoint: the Art of Canvas Embroidery*, London 1974

Windrum, Sarah *Needlepoint*, London 1980

List of Suppliers

UNITED KINGDOM

Madeira Threads (UK) Ltd
Ryder House
Back Lane
BOROUGHBRIDGE
Yorkshire YO5 9AT

Bolton Doll & Craft Supplies Centre
Markland Street
Off Soho Street
BOLTON BL3 6AQ

Crimple Craft Ltd
107 Cold Bath Road
HARROGATE
Yorkshire HG2 0NU

Hobbycraft
39 High Street
SHANKLIN
Isle of Wight

Magpies
14 Peacock Market
LEIGHTON BUZZARD
Beds. LU7 5JH

Ann Mochrum
Bickington
BARNSTAPLE
Devon EX31 2JG

Northumbria Crafts
5 Main Street
SEAHOUSES
Northumberland NE68 7RD

Pastimes
93 High Street
HYTHE
Kent CT21 5JH

Redburn Crafts
Squires Garden Centre
Halliford Road
Upper Halliford
SHEPPERTON
Middlesex TW17 8RU

Sew-In-Seconds
Lea Road
FORRES
Morayshire
Scotland

Something Special
41 High Street
CHASETOWN
Staffs. WS7 8XE

Taurus Crafts
11 Auldbar Road
LETHAM
Scotland

Village Craft Shop
The Square
FOREST ROW
East Sussex

EUROPE

Madeira Garnfabrik Rudolf Schmidt KG
Postfach 320
7800 FREIBURG
WEST GERMANY

Kasite Ky
Hameentie 4C 10
00530 HELSINKI
FINLAND

USA

Madeira USA Ltd.
59 Primrose Drive
O'Shea Industrial Park
LACONIA
New Hampshire 03246

AUSTRALIA

Penguin Threads PTY Ltd.
25-27 Izett Street
Prahran 3181
Victoria